The
MILLENNIAL MAKEOVER

WHO ARE WE AND WHO
DO WE WANT TO BECOME?

Hailey Jordan Yatros

all my love, *Hailey*

BALBOA
PRESS
A DIVISION OF HAY HOUSE

Balboa Press books may be ordered through booksellers or by contacting:

Balboa Press
A Division of Hay House
1663 Liberty Drive
Bloomington, IN 47403
www.balboapress.com
1 (877) 407-4847

Because of the dynamic nature of the Internet, any web addresses or links contained in this book may have changed since publication and may no longer be valid. The views expressed in this work are solely those of the author and do not necessarily reflect the views of the publisher, and the publisher hereby disclaims any responsibility for them.

The author of this book does not dispense medical advice or prescribe the use of any technique as a form of treatment for physical, emotional, or medical problems without the advice of a physician, either directly or indirectly. The intent of the author is only to offer information of a general nature to help you in your quest for emotional and spiritual well-being. In the event you use any of the information in this book for yourself, which is your constitutional right, the author and the publisher assume no responsibility for your actions.

Any people depicted in stock imagery provided by Thinkstock are models, and such images are being used for illustrative purposes only.
Certain stock imagery © Thinkstock.

Printed in the United States of America.

ISBN: 978-1-4525-9089-9 (sc)
ISBN: 978-1-4525-9091-2 (hc)
ISBN: 978-1-4525-9090-5 (e)

Library of Congress Control Number: 2014901254

Balboa Press rev. date: 02/04/2014

This could be a must-read inspiring book for the millennial generation—the generation that will influence and control world decisions well into the next couple of decades. It will also provide an understanding for parents/caretakers so that they can communicate more effectively with their young people.

As a member of the millennial generation myself, my intention with this book is to help my peers (and possibly their parents) start

- leading instead of following;
- loving instead of hiding;
- embracing instead of running; and
- having undeniable confidence in ourselves.

While reading this book, you, the millennial, will be reminded that love and connection is still the only way to attain deep fulfilling relationships, both with yourself and with the important people in your life. Technology has deprived us of human connection. It has taken away our sense of the importance of being close to people. So my message is, how can we use it as a tool for success instead of as a social safety buffer?

I will encourage you to discover your purpose and then do whatever it takes to achieve it. After reading this book, you will stop doubting yourself and, as a result, start to trust your abilities as a young adult to fulfill the purpose that touches your heart. College isn't the only way to do that. It's important to march to your own drummer and ignore the critics. There will always be someone out there who will doubt you and try to crush your enthusiasm.

Ladies and gentlemen, start loving yourselves in order to live the life you've always dreamed about. Begin the journey and work at eliminating self-doubt. Explore what success means to you, and know that you are the rising leaders of our generation and the next.

This book has it all for millennials. Make technology work *for* you, not *through* you. Learn that love and connection are still the only ways to have a fulfilling life. Use your youth as an advantage instead of an excuse. Celebrate your own uniqueness and follow your heart so that you can be successful in your own way.

My ultimate message is that we only have

    one life,
    one soul,
    one chance.

Let's make it count!

"Hailey Jordan is a bright light in a dark world. Her heart for God and good pours out in the wisdom she shares on the pages of *The Millennial Makeover*.

There is no greater power than the "love" in this book. It clearly gives every reader a better life, and thus a better world!"

Susie Dahlmann- Teacher- Trainer and Christ Servant- Co-founder of Reaching Higher: "Leadership Training for a better world."

Contents

Foreword

Who Is This Young Author?

Is Hailey a remarkable young woman? Yes indeed! She is wise way beyond her age. What Hailey is attempting to do is to reach her peers and give them hope, and anyone else who is older and interested in making something of themselves, rather than feeling stagnant. In this book, she depicts a generation that is faced with multiple obstacles, both emotionally and situationally. And yet Hailey is full of hope and enthusiasm to encourage young people to not give up—that they can still have dreams, that they can still plan and move beyond their individual circumstances.

I have known Hailey for the past five years, as her therapist and subsequently, after she completed her therapy goals, as her mentor as she embraces this passion of hers. I cannot say that she has overcome more unusual obstacles than the average teen. Actually, her history of fighting to be heard is very typical of our young people today, and yet not typical, because she has not accepted that her future is hopeless; she consistently fought to go beyond feeling discouraged and/or defeated.

As I read Hailey's book, I was continually amazed at the insight this young girl has and her relentless quest to show love and acceptance for others. She is unusually intelligent in her ability to express herself and represent her generation. Her book is so intricately clear in this representation that it leaves no doubt on how to overcome the obstacles our young people may face. To achieve this end, Hailey provides sections with specific questions at the end of the chapters so that the reader can examine his/her thoughts. This gives the reader a chance to stop and think about how he/she can integrate and use the information.

Hailey explains in detail how it is very difficult for a young person to step aside his/her generation and see into the future of his/her next generation. But this is exactly what Hailey has done herself. And with this book, Hailey demonstrates and gives her readers an example of how forgiveness/love can be a concrete instrument to guide them in going beyond their circumstances to live a life that is full of promise and hope.

As an adolescent and looking back at her childhood, she gradually discovered that what she thought was a loving relationship in her family was, in fact, troubled. It was not what she expected to experience—through a child's mind. It was in her late teens, and with the help of therapy and the relentless patience/love from her mother, that Hailey developed a determination to move beyond her hurt and then to help someone else do the same thing. The innocent enthusiasm and love for people that she felt and expressed as a child, has never left her, though. In spite of feeling sad and angry, she kept that fire alive to be happy and worked to overcome her family disappointments and avoid the bitterness that is so common with internal unresolved hurt.

It was also very evident to me that Hailey has been gifted and somehow guided by her intense belief in God and His ever-present hand in shaping her thoughts. It was her mother who modeled for her to always have faith in God's presence. Therefore, her unusual abundance of love can only be explained by her strong faith and trust that she is God's instrument to help others achieve their dreams. When feeling discouraged, or defeated, or rejected, she has the ability to shake it off and bounce right back—keeping her love for others constantly in the foreground. She's like the Energizer Bunny, consistently moving forward to reach out to her peers to pass out hope for their future.

Anyone who spends any amount of time with Hailey will, at one point in their experience with her, look at her with awe, because they won't quite understand how she's able to continually give off love and encouragement. And yet Hailey does have a "normal" side to her. She does get discouraged; she does get scared; she does get disappointed; she does feel inadequate from time to time; and she wonders why she is so different from her friends. But instead of feeling down on herself, she just keeps going. And as a result, I'm hoping that all her peers, whom she hopes to reach with this book, will also find some speck of inspiration and hope that they too, in their own way, will be able to find themselves loving and giving to help our world become a better place.

So in conclusion, I might add that I am proud to have known Hailey and hope that our lives will continually intertwine and be internally linked on a soul's level. Hailey shares my own personal passion for helping people feel love, acceptance of themselves and others, and as a result, true connection with our world and everyone in it. So with this, I truly believe that we are kindred spirits, even though we are almost fifty years apart in age. She has proven, through our friendship/mentorship, that age is meaningless when it comes to sharing love. The most important thing in any relationship is love/acceptance for each other and a truly honest and genuine connection, as she so vividly describes in her book. As a result then, as we connect in a genuine way, our relationship becomes ageless.

Therefore, it is my opinion that this book is not just focused on adolescents and twenty-year-olds, but everyone who is wanting something more meaningful in their life. Something that will help them wake up in the morning and look forward to being with someone that they love. Something that will help them overcome the obstacles that interfere with their need to feel loved and accepted. Something that will help them to say, "Okay, life is good," even though they may be faced with numerous trials. And even though it is impossible for a human being to live each day without trials, Hailey gives the reader *hope* with this book. Her book demonstrates that it is not impossible for a human being to seek out love, in spite of his/her circumstances, so that they can give and receive it. It just may take a little planning.

And that's what Hailey Jordan Yatros is trying to teach us all.

Susan A. Maloney, PhD
Licensed Clinical Psychologist

Acknowledgments

Someone once told me, "Hailey, people don't get successful by themselves. Other people help them get to where they want to be—that is why they have an acknowledgments section in every book."

This couldn't be truer. This book is a success because of the many individuals who have helped me make it possible. I first want to thank my entire family: my mother, for her undying faith in my abilities; my natural father, for helping me out when I needed him the most; my new stepfather, for his support and added suggestions; and all of my siblings, who shared my trials with me and collectively cheered me on when it seemed no one else was there to notice me and my discomfort. Last but not least, I want to thank the most amazing grandparents for their authentic acceptance of who I am as a person. I am forever grateful for the love of my whole family; it is indescribable.

I would like to wholeheartedly thank the remarkable millennials and parents of millennials I interviewed for this book. Thank you for taking the time to share your most vulnerable, open thoughts and ideas with me. It added tremendous value to this book. A huge thank-you to all of the wonderful individuals who have encouraged me along this journey. A special thank-you to Susan Dooley; I could never be where I am today without your love and never-ending encouragement when I started to question myself. I hope you always know your friendship has forever changed my life. I am truly grateful.

Thank you to my publishing consultant, Wendy Herrington, for your words of inspiration. You were the first and only consultant I spoke with. I knew that Balboa Press would be a perfect fit for me, because of you. I want to sincerely thank my Anthony Robbins Life Coach, Delia Knight, for her support and direction in my life. You are such a blessing and an incredible coach. You helped me make my vision a reality.

And, of course, my very best friend, my mentor, my coach, and my everything: Dr. Susan A. Maloney. I call you my guardian angel because you have guided me, loved me unconditionally, and always believed in me. We have never let our age hinder our connection, and I am so glad we never will. Thank you for taking me under your wing and being the most selfless, dedicated, incredible human being I've ever known. I love you to the moon and back.

The list goes on and on. From the bottom of my heart, I would like to thank all the people who have helped me make this book successful.

Introduction

Why Did I Write This Book?

*W*hy? is a question I've always been intrigued by. Why am I here? Why can life be so hard? Why is life full of adventure yet slowed down by fear? Why don't people realize they can choose to be happy or to be miserable? Why do bad things happen to good people? Let me share with you *why* you should continue to read this book.

First, this book is for millennials. What is a millennial? *Millennial* is the name for the twenty-first century's first generation. We are also called Generation Y.

There have been disputes on the age range for a millennial. A recent study indicates that a millennial is anyone who was born between the years 1980 and 2000, and that's the age range I'll use for this book. But I'm also talking to the parents of these millennials to give them an inside perspective on where young people today are coming from and how to leverage communication between the generations.

What I hope to offer is a new perspective into the lives of many young adults. Everything I offer in this book—every tip, every story, every bit of advice—is a result of what I have gained from my own experience. Applying these tools myself is what has made me so successful at such a young age. I have interviewed multiple millennials (ages thirteen to thirty-three) to get an even deeper perspective on how we live, what we think on a daily basis, what makes us succeed, and what stops us from growing. These amazing individuals have helped me tremendously while writing this book.

I believe that their heartfelt and honest answers will help you too. I view this life as if we are on one big team, and what a team does is help one another out when needed. That is the place I am coming from with this book, and that is why I gathered other people's viewpoints to help me. I cannot fulfill my mission without all of you, and the truth of the matter is that we can all relate to one another on some level. I've interviewed individuals from all over: from Boston to New Hampshire, from Nashville to Detroit. It just goes to show that, no matter where we are, millennials are experiencing the same things. We can learn from each other and help each other.

If you do not believe everything I suggest or choose not to apply it, that is okay. I used to read self-help books and try so hard to implement every single principle, every step-by-step. I tried to be perfect, but perfection is just not attainable. The truth is that I took away a piece here and a piece there, and it somehow had a way of coming together. If there was only one formula for success, we would all be robots, and we aren't.

This book is just a tool to help you improve and, as a result, grow your life to its highest capabilities, because even if we think we know it all, there is always room to grow. Only you can answer the question, "Why should I read this book?" What I can promise is that there is something to learn here that will improve the quality of your life. If something resonates with you, please use it, share it, experience it, and grow from it. I know it will add value to your life in some way. It is imperative that we continue to improve our lives. If we are not growing, we are dying.

From as far back as I can remember, people have called me a "spitfire." I never settled down but was constantly running to the next thing and next thing. I was a ball of energy wherever I went. What I also remember so vividly is that I truly loved people. I would say "I love you" to almost everyone and anyone who walked by me. My mother told me that when I was just three years old and about three feet tall, I would hug strangers in the grocery store and tell them I loved them. My mother had to politely tell me that it was okay to love but I shouldn't talk to strangers. But I just always had a love for others and a yearning to see other people smile and be happy. I would do just about anything for anyone growing up.

I want to begin by saying this because it stands true to this day that I sincerely have an undying love for others. And that is the underlying reason I am writing this book. I want my readers to know that everyone is a beautiful soul and that everyone has a right to be treated as such.

My goal is to, in the words of St. Francis, contribute a little bit of hope where there is despair, a little bit of love where there is hatred, a little bit of peace where there is confusion, and a little bit of faith when there is fear. I am certain that as you continue to read and apply what you have read, you will be able to conquer anything you may face in your lifetime. My hope in writing this book is to start breaking down the stereotypes that our society places on our generation and to shed new light on where we are coming from and what we can do as millennials to help make a new name for ourselves: to step out, step up and become who we were created to be.

The way I have set up these chapters is a little bit different. Before I loved to read, I would take one look at a huge thick book and say, "Heck no, I'm not reading that long thing!" As millennials, we are so used to having everything fast and easy. Everything is at our fingertips. That is how I designed this book. It is an easy read, and the chapters are shorter so I can keep your attention.

Inside the chapters, I have included exercises and what I call "Thinking Caps," which are a series of questions to help you think about and really apply what you are learning. I know for a fact that we cannot simply *know*—we have to *apply*. Knowledge is meaningless without action. Smack dab in the middle of the word k*now*ledge is *now*. Take action now!

To engage my readers, I've added different questions and highlighted specifics in each chapter so that you can have the most value at your fingertips. Please keep in mind that I am right here with you, reading, learning, and growing with you—going through this experience with you. I hope you always remember that we are together in learning how to be happy and satisfy our inner desire to have purpose and meaning in our lives.

I Love You,

Hailey Jordan Yatros

Chapter 1

We All Have Our Own Story

Millennials get a bad rap. Have you noticed? It's hard to pursue a career we really desire or make the money we deserve because many business owners think we don't want to work or don't have enough life experience, and some even think we are doing nothing with our lives. One major stereotype I frequently encounter is that we "get everything from our parents" and "don't want to work for anything." Go on any business site—Forbes, Entrepreneur, Inc., etc.—and search "millennial blogs." You will see the stereotypes exploding with a lot of different opinions and lessons that the millennial generation should learn.

That is fine. People are free to write what they want and think what they want. My mission is to break those stereotypes down and really get into the core truth of who we are. I am not trying to bash any other generation. I am teaching how we can cultivate success in our own lives so that we can live by pure example, so that we don't feel like we have to prove ourselves to anyone anymore.

According to a recent study, "58 percent of hiring managers said they're not planning to hire entry-level college graduates this year. And 66 percent of hiring managers said they don't think new college graduates are prepared for the workplace."[1] This rubs me the wrong way because it insinuates that millennials don't have what it takes to be hired. Granted, being hired is more difficult because of the poor economy and the way businesses are structured now, but we are the ones who are being heavily affected because we are finding fewer opportunities, have a *ton* of student debt, and possess no idea of where to go so that we can grow into responsible adults while paying our debt down.

Yet we still are optimistic about our future, and we still value meaningful relationships and care about our lives. We just need a little knowledge about how to thrive in today's times and push through what others may say about our generation as a whole. Being a millennial can be challenging sometimes. I mean, come on. We are just like everyone else, and we deserve to be treated as such. But then, sometimes it can be a blast: great opportunities, parties, prom, eating junk food and never gaining a pound, listening to loud music, laughing with your friends, sports, tailgating, college graduation, marriage, starting families, and so on. I like the name *millennials*; it reminds me of all the millions of dollars we are going to make.

Some of our parents are prodding us to go to college even if we don't think it's necessary at this time. Our lives consist of everyone telling us what to do, when to do it, and how to do it— be professional, get good grades, don't say this, act this way, be

---

[1] Max Mihelich, "College Grads, Ready or Not? Employers Think Not," *Workforce*, April 30, 2013, http://www.workforce.com/articles/college -grads-ready-or-not-employers-think-not.

home at this time, don't wear that, go to college, land that great job out of school, go into debt … I could go on and on. People put demands on our lives as if they have a say! Maybe the people we trust and respect have a say, but what about the rest of the world that wants us to "fit in" or to be a certain way? What about all those people who want us to do what *they* want?

If people only knew the daily trials we have to face. This is not a "poor me" mind-set. It is simply an awareness as to what we are thinking. Sometimes it's *so* confusing being a millennial and not knowing how to act, who you are, what you want, and if you should think this way or think that way. There are the friends, the teachers, the parents, the bosses, and everyone else telling us what to do. Oh, and let's not forget the magazines and the movies we watch with our friends that are full of what our society forces us to be. There are so many hidden expectations today in the media that unconsciously make us feel like we have to live up to them.

The stereotypes swarming around us as a generation are so unfair. We constantly feel as if we have to prove ourselves in the workplace because we are younger. Before we are even out of college, we need to have a significant amount of experience for business owners to even give us a shot. And what about the millennials who want to be successful—those of us who *are* driven and focused, who really have a heart to do something great in our world, and are criticized and hindered because of our age?

Although there are exceptions to every rule, this seems to be our reality. And how we can start to change it is to first start believing that we are more than just a generation. We are more than just people who don't want to work, and we are more than what our resumes say. What other generations don't know about us is that we have many tools and resources to help *them* out. We know how to use technology to its greatest capacity; our youth is a major advantage, not a crutch.

Since we're all individuals, we all have different experiences. And maybe you're reading about all these millennial challenges and thinking, "No, that's not true," or "I haven't experienced that yet in my life." I would still strongly urge you to keep reading, because there are some indispensable techniques and topics that I'll explore on how you can catapult yourself to a higher level than where you are already.

In order to do that, it is important to understand where we come from and to examine our stories to figure out how our origins have played a role in the lives we live today. You have a different story than I have and come from a different family, but it is just as important that you identify with your past and first go back to your story. Our stories are a big part of who we are.

Some of us have families who are there through thick and thin—moms and dads who have given us everything, loved us unconditionally, taught us how to make smart and healthy decisions, guided us toward the right direction, and all around supported us in life. On the other hand, some of us come from families who treated us poorly, looked down on us, discouraged us, pointed out every single thing we did wrong, never helped us, and consistently told us that we couldn't do what we wanted to do or what we should have done. Of course, some of us have had families that just weren't around at all. You didn't see your parents that much. They worked a lot, didn't have much to say, and rarely asked what you were feeling.

Whatever our upbringing, whether as children or in our current living situations, we can all learn, we can all grow, and we can all be successful leaders in the years to come if we just make the decision to do so. We have to start by looking at the stories of how we were raised and where we came from so that we can accept it, heal from it (if we have to), and move on to our exciting future. As I share my story with you, start thinking about your story and how it might have affected who you are today. What kinds of hurts are you holding on to that keep you from being you? How do you think your story has impacted your life? Think deeply. Start to open your mind to the creation of your dreams.

My Story

I'll go first. My story begins in a small town in Michigan. I was an outspoken kid. I always said what was on my mind when I was younger, and it frequently got me into trouble. I was raised in what you might call a dysfunctional family, but then again, there are many families who are dysfunctional in their own way. When I was ten years old, my mother told me that my stepfather at the time wasn't my biological dad, that she didn't know where my biological father lived, and that she didn't have contact with him because they had split up when they were younger.

My childhood was anything but an easy road; it was a life of struggle, and my successes were not just handed to me. Many times I felt like the protector of my family, because I was always the most assertive. I tried to take care of my siblings emotionally, and it became a burden that was heavy to carry. Growing up without my real father in my life was a true battle, because a lot of the time, I felt as if I had to do everything on my own, and I could never really rest.

Time and time again, I felt as if I had to fight for my freedom as a child. I had no control over anything, and all I really yearned for was love. As more and more discouragement came my way, I grew stronger and stronger. Little did I know that I was building up wall after wall, stuffing down feelings on top of other feelings.

My mother is a saint. She has compassion for others that I've never seen before. Although my mother is a sensational woman, she was emotionally limited, and as a result I continuously felt alone. On the other hand, I feel as if my mother's love for me was the only thing that got me through. She is an amazing woman who has a strong faith, but unfortunately her fear overruled her faith when I was growing up. I watched as my mother put her real feelings and voice into her shell, leaving her feeling powerless. All she has ever wanted was peace in her family, love for her kids, and for someone to love her and her children.

I felt as a child like I was walking on eggshells and anything I said would be wrong or shot down. This made me not sad but angry, and over the years I started to become a very angry young adult. After a series of interesting events, at age fifteen I met my biological father. It was at that time that I realized the severity of my anger and how much it was holding me back from having the life that I always dreamed of. With the help of my mother, I began attending therapy and kept with it until I finally learned to release my anger and start to soar toward my dreams.

It was during my time in therapy that I began to turn my life around. Then, without even realizing it at the time, I noticed that things started to go extremely well for me in a very short period of time. As I started to progress into my adult years, I realized how my age was really affecting the way people treated me. I had entered the business world at age eighteen, faced a lot of trials, and constantly had to overcome credibility issues with other professionals and adults. This frustrated me because I felt like it was holding me back, and I always thought I had to wait to be successful until I was "older" and had more "life experience."

After attending a live Tony Robbins seminar when I was nineteen, I signed a contract with a life coach. It was, and still is, one of the best choices I've ever made. She told me to start asking myself how I could be resourceful, as opposed to thinking that my age was a problem. Then one day, my vision vividly became so real for me that I had to do something about it. I knew then that I had to put my passion on paper. This idea became the focus for my book, stemming from my own frustration over being "heard," but also from my passion for helping young adults like myself succeed in life and avoid any stereotypes that might hold them back from making their dreams come true.

The road to discovering my passion wasn't easy. There were moments when I experienced pure joy, when I felt more love than I ever had before. I am aware that there are plenty of other individuals who have experienced far worse than I ever did. I just want to be clear that I did not have an easy road; success was not handed to me on a silver platter. I had to work hard, love hard, and believe in myself to press through all of the hurts that I experienced. I know there is someone out there who will read this book, at least *one* person, who will become a better person from my experiences, and that is enough for me.

Your Story

Although I do not know who you are, I do know that you have a story too. What is your story like? What were your parents like? Do you feel confident about your future because of how you grew up? Have you had some hard times? How about the fun times? What is an amazing memory you will never forget? Write down some of the crucial moments in your life that made you who you are today. Even if it's one thing, go ahead and write some of the answers to these questions down.

We don't have to live in our past (I'll talk more about that in chapter 13), but it is important to realize that how you grew up has a big impact on the desires that you have for your life today. And you still may be in the process of "growing up." You may not think you have any desires or a care in the world, but your past still has an influence on what you think and feel today.

Our past experiences have a lot to do with the development of our personality and who we will become. However, we don't have to allow those experiences to define who we are. Okay, this is the only time I'm going to tell you to stop reading and really think about your story. Jot down memories you have that are important to you. Write down exciting memories, painful memories, memories where you experienced a lot of laughter, or memories with a lot of tears, whatever you want. Write at least a couple. Go!

So I just have to trust that you have written down some of these answers. Now, what I want you to do is throw that piece of paper away like you have never thrown a piece of paper away before! *Tear* it up, *rip* it up, *run* it under water, *shred* it, do whatever you want. Just get *rid* of it! Everything in your life up to the point of you reading this book is gone; you will never get it back again. Stay with me as I uncover some of the most important truths we can know as a generation and as individuals.

> *Change is the law of life. And those who look only to the past or present are certain to miss the future.*
> —John F. Kennedy

Okay, now let's turn our eyes to the future (the next page) and start to prepare something exciting for you.

Chapter 2

Opportunities for Millennials

B eing a millennial myself, I would be lying if I said I haven't checked my cell phone at least five times while writing this chapter. Let's face it: technology has advanced at an unimaginable pace over the years and still is advancing more rapidly than we can ever imagine. Today, more iPhones are sold in a day than babies are born! There are over 1.8 million smartphones being made a day, and by the time you pick up and read this book it will probably be more than that.

It is no secret that technology runs our world , and even though it is an aggravating thing sometimes when you lose a signal or power, it is still fascinating. Now, let me specify what I mean by technology: our cell phones, our computers, our Kindles, our iPods, and even more specifically, Facebook, Twitter, Vine, YouTube, LinkedIn, Instagram, and so many others that I am probably missing.

Technology has given us so many gifts. Answers are at our fingertips because of Google. I am horrible with directions, and because of Siri and GPS, I can relax and know that I will get to where I am going without ever having to read a map. I can connect with people through pictures and chats. We have so many "i's" nowadays: iMacs, iPhones, iPods, iPads. We have sync in our cars and on our phones. You see? Technology is involved in every aspect of our lives. There is nothing that technology is not involved in, and that is amazing!

Do you have any idea how much easier our lives are in this generation as millennials? We can't even remember the days when we had to go to the Yellow Pages to find a phone number or search for hours to find answers to simple questions that you can now just ask your computer. Heck, my mom still remembers when computers weren't around and it took her hours to find a piece of research. Let me just give you a picture:

Millennials	Our Parents
• Google	• Library
• Cell phones	• Phone book, one family phone, pay phones
• Computers	• Books
• Online marketing, Internet	• Fliers, word of mouth
• Flat screens, BlueRay, color TV	• VCRs just came out
• Easier opportunities	• Harder to find opportunities
• GPS	• Paper maps

It's no secret that we're growing up in thriving times. And in a way, we have it much easier than our parents did, considering everything we ever need is right at our fingertips all the time. I mean, come on, could you imagine waiting to make a call on the family phone? That is no way we would live today!

My point with all of this is that we do not realize how many opportunities we have with technology. There are so many doors open for us when we live in a day and age of online marketing, where you can buy or sell anything online. On YouTube, people are becoming famous by simply uploading a video and getting so much exposure in the form of views. We can even read and write books online. There are templates to have our own website, there are blogs we can find and read specific information to feed our minds, and finally, there's Facebook, which as everyone knows is there to stay connected with our friends.

The normal person living today cannot even begin to wrap his or her mind around how powerful the Internet alone is, and that's just one piece of technology. What about our cars? Look how advanced they have become, with wireless speakers, Bluetooth— you name it, we've got it! And yet, I know I am missing a lot.

The issue is that we heavily rely on technology for everything, even in our casual relationships and close friendships. Technology can be thought of as a weapon; it can be used to kill or to create. It can kill or harm our relationships because it can distort our sense of connection with people, especially those we want to have close relationships with. We *cannot* define ourselves by how many friends we have on Facebook or how many followers we have on Twitter. I have seen so many of my friends hide behind their computer screen and then, when they try to go out in the real world and get a job, they are stunned when they can't get the career they want or the relationship they want. They become a different person when they are behind the computer screen than they are with real people face to face.

I had a friend who was completely obsessed with social media, who *loved* the Internet and all the ways to "connect" with people online. She became so obsessed that it took control of her life. When she would post things to her site and didn't get enough "likes" or "retweets," she would feel horrible. She let it affect the way she lived her life. She consistently got in fights with people on Facebook, always wrapped up in the drama; she thrived on what other people thought of her. It started to become her life. She would always lock herself into the computer and wouldn't have any social life outside of the Internet.

She started to literally make a separate life online, but it was a life focused on seeking approval from others. She cared so much about what other people thought that she wouldn't buy a shirt or make a move without seeing what her "friends" thought first. She started to express herself only in ways she thought would be pleasing to other people. The Internet world became her self-imposed personal prison.

Now what kind of life is that? A life ruled by other people? Can you relate to my friend? I used to be that way, trapped by what others thought of me. But this is the reality: we live in a society where we cannot be happy unless all of our friends approve of what we say and what we do. It's not fair how much power we give the people around us. *They* start to create our lives, not us.

Why do we do this? Why do we let our "friends" control what we think and feel and wear? It's just a little thing I like to call FEAR, which stands for Fake Emotions that Are Real. The reason I say that is because FEAR is fake—it is not true! It is just a lie, an illusion, and a reason we keep telling ourselves in order not to follow our dreams. However, it is an emotion that, in the moment, feels *so* real! It disables us emotionally from living out our purpose in life.

I could write all day on fear alone, but I'll just save that for another book. My point, though, is that fear isn't a little thing, but something that is alive and well in all of our lives. It can have so much power and control over our decisions that it can even destroy our lives if we continue to feed into it and believe it. In my interviews with my peers and through my own personal experiences, I have found that we millennials have so many fears. Most of these fears are unconscious, which means they are fears we don't consistently think about on a daily basis. Sometimes they are fears we don't even know we have! *And yet they control our lives.*

When I started my first real corporate job, I was so nervous. At the time, I was so young and terrified of what others would say or think when I walked in. Would they take me seriously? Would people listen to my ideas? Could I prove to them that I had what it takes? I was so fearful on my first day that when I was in the parking lot, I ended up turning around and saying I was sick. I ultimately was afraid of rejection and of what others would think of me. I was severely terrified of failure and also success.

This is the kind of fear I am talking about: the fear that takes over your life. You are blinded by what you are becoming. You have put up such a façade that *you* don't even know the real you. We all have fears about not being enough, about other people not accepting our real selves, so we hide, we run, we *lie* to "fit in." I know this because that was me. I was the girl who was mean to other people because I was hurting deep down inside. I thought I had to make fun of others to make myself feel better.

Technology is great until we let it control our lives. Then it becomes a mask we hide behind and use to become someone else. We have more courage on the Internet because we can use it to hide our real selves, and in the underground faceless network of technology we can say what we want to say, we can be mean, we can start drama, and then we can just delete it if we want. Bullying has always been a major issue in our society, but now with the Internet expanding, it is getting even worse.

Young adults should *not* be dying because of the words we say to one another. This is another truly sad and tragic thing about technology and how we abuse it. It can be a very dangerous world online. We need to protect ourselves and also make sure that we are using technology as a resource to build others up, not tear them down. Online can be a scary place, so stay alert for traps that you know are bad for you. Pretend you are talking to an audience of a hundred people sitting in front of you listening to every word.

Sometimes, being a young adult hurts. You might be thinking, *Me? No, I'm not hurt, I am just fine.* But what I mean is that emotionally, we may ache inside. We are denying to ourselves how we really feel, and then we find ourselves hiding from this hidden truth. We hurt so deeply sometimes that we want other people to feel our pain. We just want *someone* to understand who we are and where we are coming from and to listen to our pains, our complaints, our dreams, and our passions.

So we act out, in desperate need of attention, and that is where the sad stories and news articles begin. As we get older, this hurt turns into entitlement and ego. We start to believe that we are what others think of us, and we are important based on how many awards we get or how well we do in work and how successful we become.

The Solution

I have good news, though: it doesn't have to be this way. There are other ways to be heard, and we can still enjoy technology to its fullest while having real friends and committed relationships. Opportunities surround us more than we can ever imagine. We live in such a thriving time, and there are abundant ways to make money and have amazing friendships by using the Internet as a tool instead of letting technology use us. Here are some tips on how to use technology to your advantage.

Be strategic with the Internet

Having a lot of connections on social-media sites is a great thing because we branch out, reach people we never thought we could, and keep in touch with people we don't see very often. These are just a few of the many ways in which it is a huge plus—just as long as we don't use it to define *who we are*.

I had a breakthrough one day after reading an article. I started to use the Internet to my *advantage*. I started purposely selecting who I wanted on my social-media sites and with whom I wanted to stay connected. I started to be strategic about what I wanted to post— what I wanted my message to the world to be. My posts changed from complaining about my life to empowering people to live better lives. I started posting quotes that inspired me, and I started to weed out all the people who didn't make me a better person.

Being strategic opened the door of opportunities for me. I started to connect with businesspeople, people who made me smarter, and people who could open doors for me to make money. You never know who you will meet and who will help you. In fact, that is how I got three job interviews for high-paying jobs right after graduating from high school.

Don't let Facebook or any other social media control you, and don't use others as your punching bag. Social-media sites are not meant to be used to abuse others and tear them down. It's just wrong. Use them for working, uplifting people, and finding new opportunities. Let them be a resource for helping others and being successful.

Use technology as an instrument for research

There is so much information online. Use it to your benefit! Instead of looking at Vine videos for three hours or stalking people on Facebook, learn how to play the guitar on YouTube, get educated in the career you want to go into, look up blogs about health or photography or other things you love, create a blog, watch inspirational videos on YouTube, read a good book. You can Google anything and get the answer right away.

Whenever I open my laptop and before I get onto any social-media site, I watch a video that makes me feel empowered or read an article that I can learn something from. Find something that you're interested in and research it. Get educated about what you enjoy and become a master at it. Soak up all the knowledge you can, because you will be able to use it as a major advantage in your life. The more knowledge you can gain at a young age, the more you will be taken seriously for what you believe in.

Limit your use of technology

As much as I love my cell phone and computer—and I really love them—I know I have to be disciplined to limit my time spent on them. Have you ever been on Facebook or your cell phone and realized that three hours have passed? I have! You can easily get sucked into spending too much time on the Internet and not get one thing done. Give yourself a limit—maybe it's only two hours of the Internet a day, or maybe you don't even spend that much time on your phone or computer, in which case limit it to an hour and instead go out with a friend, spend time with your family, exercise, read or write. Whatever it may be for you, you will soon find fulfillment in your life that the Internet could never give you.

Thinking-Cap Time!

1. How much do you let technology control your world? On a scale of 1–10 (1 being *hardly ever* to 10 being *I can't get enough*), how much time do you spend on some piece of technology?

   _____

2. What are two ways you can utilize technology to help you get ahead?

   _____

   _____

3. What will you do differently as a result of reading this chapter?

   _____

   _____

   _____

What Have We Learned So Far?

- We learned that technology is an amazing thing and that it's the reason we have so many advantages living in today's time.

- We recognized that technology can be used for much more than just posting pictures.
- We already knew that we could have a lot of fun with technology, but we now know that we need to be careful about how we use it—let's be productive! There are endless possibilities for us to be successful and stay connected online.
- We learned that fear is very real and alive in our lives and that it may be the reason we hide behind technology: we may have a tendency to be afraid to reveal our true self.
- We learned that leveraging technology could be an easy avenue toward success.

Since the beginning of our lives—since we were babies—we have instinctively known the importance of human connection. We strive with all our might to make a connection. Have you ever seen a week-old infant? Next time you do, notice how that child gazes into the eyes of other people. Infants just stare because they are receiving connection with another person, which is vital for their survival.

That intense need to connect is still vital for our survival today. We never outgrow it. We will always seek connection with other humans, and that is something technology cannot give us. It is the very reason we yearn for connection with others and rely too much on technology to achieve it. Sometimes, it can lead us down a dangerous and dark path without us even knowing it. Use it, don't abuse it!

It has become appallingly obvious that our technology has exceeded our humanity.
—Albert Einstein

Chapter 3

Love Is the Only Way
(and No, I'm Not Talking about Sex)

We came into this world to love and be loved.
If we can remember that, everything else will work out.

When you see the word *love*, what comes to your mind? Is it a dozen roses? A kiss? A hug? Is it the expression of a touch or a smell? Is it hearing someone say, "I love you"? When you think of love, do you think of sex? If you only pay attention to one thing this whole book, make it this: there is a *huge* difference between love and sex. Some of you may associate love with the mushy gushy sentiment that you never want to think or talk about, but what I am referring to here is the love that created you and I in the first place, so just keep an open mind.

First, let's travel along the journey of love. It's one of my favorite topics to talk about because I feel so strongly about it. After you have read the questions above, you may be thinking about what love means to you. Whatever that may be, it's okay. Your thoughts about love are not wrong. To begin, I would like to share with you my own outlook on love.

It is my opinion that love can be expressed without saying a word, feeling a touch, or even being near someone. Love is an infinite force in our world that we all seek. Our spirits are love. We were born into innocent pure love, and that has been the basis of our life, whether we realize it or not. Have you ever gone on a trip where you left your parents or your siblings or your friends behind? Well, when you went away, you didn't stop loving them; you were just away from them. That's what I mean by love. It is a force we cannot see, but we can feel it all of the time. It is a "knowing."

It is not a light switch you can turn on and off. When love is there—when true love is present—it never goes away. It continues to burn like a candle that could never be blown out. Love is inside all of us to give, to give to ourselves first and foremost. And I don't mean to imply that this is a selfish act of love. No, on the contrary, we cannot give away what we don't already have inside of us. Therefore, to love ourselves by protecting ourselves from harm, whether physical or emotional, is loving ourselves so that we can feel fulfilled to love others. It is honoring the love that is already inside of us so that we can give it away.

If you ask to borrow five dollars from someone, and they only have three dollars in their hands, it's not that they don't want to give you the five dollars; they simply don't have five dollars to give. It's the same with love. If you don't first love yourself and cherish yourself, you cannot possibly love another human being.

So what does it look like to love yourself? Before I give my answer, I want to share opinions and understandings on this topic from some other millennials; they might resonate with you too.

- "Do what makes you happy or what's best for you, because you cannot take care of anyone else if you don't take care of yourself first. You have to love yourself before you can ever love anyone else."—Hero, 26
- "Constantly give yourself pep talks. What you say to yourself when you're having a bad day: that really defines how much you love yourself."—Kara, 24
- "When you can walk away from a situation that does not bring you closer to success."—Maeghan, 24
- "First and foremost you have to love yourself before anyone else."- Anonymous, 20

Loving yourself can come in many different forms and can happen in many different ways. One way is taking care of yourself by exercising and eating foods that are nutritious for you—like fruits and vegetables, plus lots of water—which will make you have more energy. Loving yourself also consists of treating yourself kindly and with respect, not putting yourself down, not calling yourself names, not thinking you're fat, ugly, not pretty enough, not thin enough, not this enough, not that enough, just plain old *not enough*. That's not loving yourself, that's hurting yourself. And if you continue down that path, you're asking for a life that's miserable and lonely. You'll never be able to treat others with kindness if you think badly of yourself.

At one point in my life, I was very angry. I was angry at the world, at my parents, my friends, and most importantly, at myself. I felt a deep sense of guilt and shame about my life, and those two ugly feelings took over. I was always rude to people; no one respected me, and if they did it was because they were afraid of me, which isn't the same as earning someone's respect.

Because I was full of anger, my life was full of anger. People responded angrily to me, and I never understood until the day someone stopped me and said, "You know, if you were just a little nicer to people, maybe you wouldn't have so many problems going on in your life." Sounds like common sense right? Well, not to me … but one day I remembered that moment, and it finally clicked with me. The people around me didn't change, but *I* changed. My insides changed first, and then my environment drastically changed.

Until we can realize that everything starts with a shift in us and a change in our attitude, we will never change. I know this because it happened inside of me. I wasn't willing to let go and change my attitude from bitter and angry to loving and kind. Once I did that, my whole life changed, and so did the people around me. So when I say loving ourselves is important, what I really mean is that it is the only way to have a joyful fulfilled life, full of amazing relationships, successful careers, and dreams.

Start Loving Yourself

To clarify my new perspective on loving yourself, I am just quickly going to jot down some changes that helped me and that you can make in order to start taking steps toward really loving and respecting yourself.

Write down one thing every day that you like about yourself, and focus on that one thing all day

There is always something you can find about yourself that you like. If you try hard and still can't find something, ask someone you like and respect, like a parent or someone you trust. Are you funny? Are you kind? Are you giving? Do you make other people smile? Are you good at writing? Singing? Dancing? Sports? Whatever it may be for you, focus on that and, most importantly, write it down and carry it with you.

Every morning you wake up, look in the mirror and say something positive about yourself

I used to do this with myself when I felt insecure and had hardly any confidence. I would say things like, "You are beautiful," "You are strong," "You have unshakable confidence," "I love you," "You are smart," "You make the right decisions for your life." You are more than welcome to use these, or you can find ones that work for you. If success is more of what you want, you may say something like, "I am success," or "Success is coming my way today." It may sound cheesy at first, and it will feel weird. But your brain and body will start to feel different, I can promise you that.

The words we say to ourselves are the most powerful tools we have over our lives. Have you ever noticed the words people use when they are having a bad day versus the people who are positive and are having a good day? You can tell by the answer to the question, "How's your day going?" A couple of answers you might hear are, "It's okay" (with a sigh) or "My day is horrible, worst day ever." On the other hand, you might hear, "My day is great!" or "I am having a terrific day!" This is a small example, but such a *huge* difference in the quality of someone's life.

So hear me when I plead with you to *watch the words you say*. Try it for one day and see the difference it makes. Even if you don't feel it at the time, when you change your words anyway, you will start to feel differently over time. This works! It's what I do every day, and you wouldn't believe the people I talk to and the opportunities that come my way.

Treat yourself with compassion

Realize that you're not going to be the best at *everything*. Everyone has his or her own unique gift to give to the world. For example, I love to sing and my best friend loves to play the piano. I couldn't play piano if my life depended on it, but my best friend plays it so beautifully. Instead of getting down on myself because I suck at piano, I'm just going to develop my gift of singing.

Whatever it is you're good at, keep doing that no matter what and forget about what you're not so good at. Treat yourself with compassion by not getting down on yourself for not being like someone else. That's loving yourself! We are all made beautifully different for a reason.

There are many other ways we can be kind and loving toward ourselves. Realize that it takes practice and practice and practice, but above all, it takes *consistency*. It takes the practice of doing this act of kindness toward ourselves, over and over again, so that we can grow stronger emotionally. We have to condition our bodies and our minds to love ourselves and find what is right about us instead of what is wrong. Once we have mastered loving ourselves, we can really truly love someone else deeply.

Let me clarify one thing here: you can love just about anyone. In fact, I would encourage loving every single person you encounter. But the love I am talking about here with you is deep love, deep-*rooted* love—to be so connected to yourself that you would never do anything to put yourself in harm's way and would never let anyone treat you worse than how you treat yourself.

Loving every person you encounter would mean doing the same thing—never causing another person harm, treating people as you would treat yourself, respecting them as you would respect yourself. It may take a few years of practice and conditioning before you can really give that deep-rooted connected love to another human being. It is only then that you can really give yourself to another person.

Sex ≠ Love

Which brings me to the other part of this chapter. Let's explore the topic of sex and what it means to our generation. When I said that humans seek love and connection more than anything else on earth, this is very true. But sometimes we millennials mistake sex for love, especially as teenagers. Now, let's get one thing straight: I am not here to say, "Don't have sex" and "Don't do drugs." I'm not writing this book to tell you to do or not to do *anything*, but rather to offer a new perspective on life and on the touchy subject of sex.

It has been my experience that as young teenagers, we misconstrued the subject of sex. We tended to use it as a game with each other, not knowing the underlying message of why we did that.

And again, I'm going to go back to the reason that teenagers, at some level, are hurting or fighting for acknowledgment and freedom. They want their independence so badly that they will do anything to get it, including giving up their bodies to someone else intimately when they *know* they are not ready. Or simply having sex with someone because it's a "fad" or "trend" that everyone is doing, so they think, "Hey, let's do it too." This is just another reminder that if we do not truly love ourselves and aren't connected to who we are, we shouldn't be having sex with others. We should be focused on taking care of ourselves and showing ourselves self-respect.

Our peer group, the people we hang around with, is who we become. It is so important that we know this truth, and I'll write more about that in future chapters. Another reason we sleep with someone who we are not in love with could be because our friends are doing it too. You may follow along because you're afraid you'll be called a prude or crude names if you don't follow the crowd.

Women who have had challenges with their dad growing up tend to fall into this trap. I know, because I was one of them. Ladies who grow up without a present father or with a father figure who didn't treat them like a princess may feel anger, bitterness, or rejection—and as a result, may be so starved for love that they look in other places to get it, including sex. They mistake having sex with someone as a sign of love when it is not, not when you're that young. Maybe you have the same fear as I did—fear of being unwanted or rejected—so you will do anything not to feel that way, or you will fall into the trap of peer pressure and have sex in order to feel cool or to block the pain of hurt and wounds from childhood.

I need to be clear that sex is a very different experience when it comes to young adolescent men and women. Women view it as something completely different than men do, and this can really complicate things even more. Some young adults may feel so insecure with themselves, so scared to show who they really are, that they use sex as their outlet to escape the reality of their feelings.

So I would like to offer to you a new perspective on sex. Think of two souls coming together instead of two bodies. Sex should be something that you only share with someone who you are truly in love with. Think of sex as a gift you want to give to your husband or your wife. Until you are truly in love with someone, you should not be using your body as a tool. It will backfire on you and leave you feeling even more lonely and sad.

Sex should be something very sacred in our lives, but unfortunately it has been and can be used as a game. Sex is not a game, and it shouldn't be used as one. It is my opinion and one of my core values that it is something that should be saved until you are in a partnership and/or married to another person. I know not everyone feels the same way, and that is totally fine. My hope is simply that you respect yourself enough to wait until you are completely grown and own your emotional maturity.

My encouragement for you would be that if you are thinking about having sex with another person, just ask yourself, "Do I love myself? Do I absolutely feel connected to who I am? Do I love myself so much that I wouldn't want to do any harm to me, or anyone else to do harm to me?" Then ask, "Am I truly in love with this person?" If you feel even the slightest doubt, then the answer is no.

Go back up to the first part of this chapter and revisit the parts about loving yourself and the things you can do to feel at peace with your decisions. These questions are really valid at any time of your life, and you can always revisit them. Your answers may change. Just remember, life always starts with love: loving yourself, loving people, and loving your life. Love gives, lust takes. That's a perfect example of the difference between love and sex.

Love is always within us, lying dormant,
waiting for us to wake it up and let it come alive.

Chapter 4

The Awkward Stage for Both Parents and Teens

"**H**ailey, it's time for us to have the talk."

"The *talk*?"

Do you remember that line? Didn't your heart just sink when you heard that? The first thing that came to my mind was, *Awkward! Eeww! Gross! Leave me alone!*

Maybe you haven't heard it yet, and maybe you never did or never will. Regardless, we all know the topic and conversation is one word: awkward! Can I just say that one more time? *Awkward!* No teenager or even adult likes to hear a discussion of sex, or really anything personal, coming from your parent.

But what if we never had this conversation growing up? What if our parents never brought it up or plan on bringing it up? Or better yet, we *lie* when we are asked whether we have had sex, if we are being safe, and all the other questions they ask. Listen, I know it's weird; it's awkward, it's uncomfortable, and frankly, I just got mad when the topic was brought up. However, this chapter goes way beyond "the talk." Sex is not the topic I want to discuss here, because the truth is that the topic of sex really isn't the only thing that is awkward with our parents. Sometimes just simply communicating how we are feeling is a touchy subject.

However, I have to tell you something very important: talking with our parents is one of the most important things we can do as young adults. I know this now, being older, so let me give you a piece of wisdom. Our parents can only help us as much as we *let them*. They can only give to us as much as we *let them*. I have the best relationship with my mother and father now simply because I started to talk to them. Trust me, it wasn't always this way, but I am letting you in on a secret before you waste precious time with your own parents.

One thing I wish I'd known when I was younger was that our parents love us so much. They really do. It's that simple. They want to give to you, love you, help you, encourage you, and more. Even if you don't think so at all or don't *feel* it at all, please believe me, they do.

When I was in the sixth grade, I got caught smoking with a friend. My mother came to pick me up from a friend's house and I had just got done smoking, so I sat in the backseat where she wouldn't smell me. She asked, "Why are you sitting in the backseat?"

I replied, "Because I am mad at you."

She politely said, "Bullshit, you're lying to me. The school called and said there have been rumors going around that you have been smoking with the eighth-graders."

I said, "That is a lie."

She threatened to go and give me a test; I was young and naïve, so I confessed and told her the whole truth. Her reply was that I was grounded for two months.

"Two months?!" It was like torture to me, especially because my best friend lived only two houses away from me. Every single day I begged my mom to let me go hang out with her. My mother told me that I was never to see that friend again, and I was forbidden to ever hang out with her again. You can imagine how I felt. My friend was like my whole world at the time. I hated my mom. Looking back, I know I didn't hate her but it sure felt like I did. I was furious and refused to speak to her for a long time.

I cut off my friendship, still so mad at my mom. As the years passed, I watched my friend go down a very bad path. When we moved up to high school, she got into some major drugs and her life started to become a long list of bad choices. We rarely spoke in high school, but needless to say I went a couple years ago and thanked my mother for what she did when I was young, and I apologized to her for the way I acted toward her. It took a lot of courage, but I did it and felt amazing afterward.

We don't realize it at the time, but usually our parents are looking out for our best interests. We may not understand *why*, but we have to trust that they love us and know what they are doing. Nevertheless, they won't be able to help us grow and be successful if we don't talk to them or tell them anything. Parents are there to love us, to help us, and to guide us, and we have to be able to tell them how we are feeling and what we are thinking so that they can help us to the best of their ability. It is going to take vulnerability and courage, and it *is* going to be awkward at times, but I can promise you that your parents crave your love just as much as you crave love from your parents. Willingness to have open communication with your parents greatly increases their trust in you and allows you to do more grownup activities.

This doesn't mean that we let our parents take care of us or give us everything we ask for, especially as teenagers. That is our time to start finding out what we want in life, what we're great at, what we love to do. It is the time to start our own life separate from our parents. We have to be willing to put in the effort of working hard to find our goals and dreams in life without our parents. They are there to support us and love us no matter what, but they can't do everything for us or give us everything. You are your own person and have a separate plan for your life than they do; you need to follow yours. There are times when my parents offer me some advice and I just smile and say thank you, and I still do what I feel in my heart to be right for me.

Forgive Your Parents

When my birthfather and I didn't speak for almost a year, I wrote him a letter. I was sixteen at the time. I'd like to share with you a little bit of that letter:

> I don't think you realize that all I ever needed was your love and trust. If you were anywhere in your life, broke, poor, dirty and had nothing to offer me but love I would've taken it in a heartbeat, because that was all I ever longed for my entire life. I've made a lot of mistakes, I know. But it doesn't define the person I am, because I really am a great person.

I wanted to share that so you could see I went through the same fights that you may be going through right now, and it is okay to be angry. You just can't let anger control your life. Learn how to forgive and accept.

Now, I may be talking to readers who don't have their parents in their lives, or don't have the support and love they need from their parents. That is where acceptance and mentorship comes in. The acceptance part is forgiving your parents for the hurt you feel from them—accepting that you cannot change them or change the circumstances in your life.

I had to do this, and it was hard. It was very hard for me to forgive my stepfather growing up for all the hurt he caused me, but it was the most freeing feeling I have ever experienced in my life. I felt as if I was just starting my life at that very moment, because the truth is that when we hold on to bitterness and anger, we are only damaging our spirit. It stops every opportunity from coming our way.

We will be trapped inside our self-imposed prison of anger forever until we forgive people who have hurt us. Our parents might be the hardest people to forgive on this planet. They were for me. Once we can do that, we can forgive anyone.

Think of forgiveness as a tool for achieving peace. People can steal from you, beat you, talk down to you, and take everything away from you, but what they cannot take from you is your *choices*. Just like we can choose whether to drink a can of pop or a glass of water, we can choose to be angry or we can choose to forgive. This choice really is only yours to make, but I am telling you that I have lived on both sides, and the side of forgiveness is the only thing that saved my life.

Sometimes young adults walk around in this bubble, ignoring everyone and sometimes feeling irritated. All our parents are trying to do is get inside of our hearts. They want to love us, they want to care for us and protect us, they want to heal our deepest wounds, and they want us to talk to them. We just have to let them in.

Sharing Perspectives

I've included some words from different adults (parents) who want to share messages with us. I believe if you only knew what they have to say, it would make your relationships better with them. I asked parents of all different ages, male and female, this question: "What is one thing you would really want your kids to know?" Some answers that I received were very touching to me. If we would just have open minds and hearts, we might be able to see their viewpoint.

- "I think the one thing parents and teenagers have in common, the one thing that they are both thinking, is 'If you could just know what it is like for me in this moment right now. And if you would just listen to me.' We are both saying the *same* thing."—Lori, 47
- "That they are the author of their own experience of life, both in the creation and perception of it. By choosing to perceive it in the best possible way, they will eventually create it to be that way. I've been coaching my daughter over lunch for a few years now and am amazed at the changes she's created for herself."—Kevin, 52
- "That I love him. That is the most important thing to me. That he knows that he is loved and that I am proud of him."—Melanie, 30

- "That I love them! That I will always be there for them. Whenever they need me, no matter what, they can always count on me! True beauty is inside of you, it doesn't matter how beautiful a person looks on the outside … it is what is inside that will show through."—Denise, 51
- "You can be anything you want to be and do anything you want to do if you want it bad enough and you are willing to work hard enough. Believe in yourself, have the motivation and drive, and make it happen!"—Denise
- "I want my child to always remember to be true to themselves in any situation in life and not to pretend to be somebody they are not. Be the best 'you' that you can be."—Robert, 48
- "This world is yours to do anything you want. Live your dreams, don't just dream them. You can do anything, never let anyone say you can't. 'I can't' or 'I don't know how' are not options. School is so important. I wish I could do it again, because I would have studied hard and not just gotten by. Don't be a bully, be a help to anyone you can. Always do your best in everything you do in life—you're only young once, every day is a day lost, tomorrow is not promised. If you lose at something, don't lose the lesson."—Mike, 44
- "I was told as a teen: love money, trust few, always paddle your own canoe. That is false! I would say to any teen today: don't believe everything you hear but seek the truth. It is okay to ask questions. Take a moment and realize you are smart enough to figure it out if you have a little guidance. That is allowed as a teen! (Really, even as an adult)."—Pam, 57

Although these may not be *our* parents' advice, we can still be mindful that what they have said is genuine and may be true for your parents too. So I'm encouraging you to just ask them what they think. They will tell us; we just have to be willing to listen. I would also like to add that the parents that I interviewed jumped at the opportunity to answer this question because they felt so deeply about us and are always willing to help out and give whenever they can.

Since this chapter is for parents as well as adolescents, I thought it would only be sensible to incorporate some of the teenagers' perspectives on life and what they want to share with their parents. I asked them the same question: "What is one thing that you want your parent to know or to understand about you?"

- "I know that you are in charge, but just because I'm young doesn't mean I'm not responsible or not capable of doing stuff. You can trust me that I will do my very best and I won't let you down."—Erynn, 13
- "That I care, I really do, and I take everything to heart, and I mean *everything*! I really try hard to do my best."—Makenzie, 15
- "To my parents, I feel like I grew up as a lost soul, because I feel like I didn't have any guidance growing up. I think that if my parents were more involved I would have more of a direction for my life."—Heather, 19
- "I love you, Mom, and I am not a baby anymore."—Domenick, 13
- "I want my parents to know that I love them so much! And regardless of how tough my childhood was, I know they did their best to keep us happy! And I am happy and I feel very independent."—Mallory, 18

I also wanted to add two more viewpoints of older millennials, so that you can get a perspective when you are doing forward thinking. I thought these answers were very relevant to this chapter:

- "I had to make my own mistakes. As much as they wanted me to do what they wanted and what they thought was best, I had to fall first, then pick myself back up."— Sarah, 25
- "I would want them to know that they have raised me to their utmost ability, to be the woman I am today. Everything that is instilled within me is because of their guidance. Therefore, if I make mistakes or do things that they may question, I am doing it for a *reason*."— Elizabeth, 21

After hearing all of these different perspectives and feelings, I've realized that there is so much common ground between parents and teens that we don't comprehend and appreciate until we're older. It doesn't have to be "awkward" to talk to our parents and other caring adults in our lives; we just need to hope they will accept us where we are coming from. We shouldn't have to wait until so many years have passed to change the way we act, speak, or think toward our parents or teenagers. These can be some of the best years if we want them to be.

Combining every conversation from either a parent or teen, and being young myself, I have created a letter expressing (from the eyes of a teen) what we would hope parents hear from us.

Dear Mom and Dad,

Sometimes we get a lot of crap for being in the generation that we were born into. But what I would beg for you to hear from us is this:

Hear our hearts, and really truly try to understand what we go through on a daily basis and how much added pressure we have growing up in this era. No, this is not a pity letter; this is simply a perspective of a day and a sneak peek into the mind of a teenager. Sometimes we wake up, if we ever did fall asleep that night, not knowing who we are, if we belong, what we should wear to school (wondering what our friends might think). Most of the time, we are usually pissed off that we even had to wake up this early, and some of us dread going to school.

On the other hand, some of us wake up feeling alive! We wake up excited to go to school and learn, or to play in that sports game we have today. Some of us are actively involved in our school and enjoy being there. Whichever way we wake up, we still feel daily struggles, we still try to see where we belong, with what clique in school: jocks, geeks, artists, popular, band or choir kids. Sometimes we just don't know.

We try to get a sense of meaning in our life. We have you guys giving us guidance about what we should do; we have our teachers' influence and their opinion; and we have our friends. Most of the time we will listen to our friends over anybody. We just want to have fun. We are usually thinking of the next dance or school event or the next test we have to study for, and it can get overwhelming. Some of us are trying to find after-school jobs because we want to save up to buy a car when we finally get our license.

Some of us have daily self-image struggles, and we don't feel pretty enough or skinny enough or muscular enough or tall enough. And if we don't look like the other people walking through the halls, we may feel insecure and hide our true selves. We are simply trying to find our place in this world.

What we need more than at any other time in our lives is to be unconditionally loved by you. We need your full presence with us when we are talking and telling you about our day and our fun teenager stuff. We need your understanding even when you cannot relate at all. We need your support even when we make the wrong choices in life. We need you to be there. We need your protectiveness (to a certain degree). We also need your tough love sometimes when you have to tell us no. And even though we are afraid to admit this, we need you to tell us to get off our butts and get a job and start our lives!

We want you to know that we love you so much and know you are doing the best you know how to do with what you're given. We forgive you for all of the hurt that has happened to us. We want you to know that you can trust everything will work out with us and that you're doing a great job. We look up to you more than we think you realize. We need you in so many ways, but if all we have is your love, then that is enough. We understand we need to be compassionate toward you too because we know you have sacrificed a lot for us; we just weren't around to see it. We thank you for all of your hard work and for understanding us.

Love always,

Us

Chapter 5

You Were Born on Purpose

Why are you holding this book right now? Why are you breathing and alive today? Relax, I am not attacking you. I am just really curious as to why you think you are alive today. Maybe you have never given it any thought. Maybe you just *know* that you were placed on earth to be a doctor, a lawyer, a singer, or whatever it may be. And maybe you're just like, who cares? Either way, I want to let every single soul reading this book know that *there is a reason you are here.*

There is a very specific reason for your existence on planet earth. Everyone, and I mean everyone, has a purpose in this world! I believe that to my very core. You were created to do great things in life. And the "great thing" doesn't have to compare in importance to anybody else's "great thing." You just have to start believing it for it to happen to you too.

Out loud, right now, no matter where you are, say this: "There is a great purpose for my life." Come on, say it just once. I don't care if it sounds cheesy at first; I am going to say again that there is power in the words we speak. I believe many millennials at a young age wonder about their purpose in life and why they are here, and they question their existence. I am not just speaking about what college to go to or what career to work in. What I am talking about here is a sense of mission to carry out here on earth and for other people.

Let's define what I mean by purpose. According to Dictionary. com, *purpose* is "the reason for which something exists or is done, made, used, etc."[2] That is what I mean. Regardless of your spiritual beliefs, I know in my heart that God has designed you for a very definite purpose: to use you to help the lives of others with your own unique gift. *Your* purpose in life stems from what you love to do on a daily basis.

Before I go any further, take a moment to either think about or write down answers to these questions. They will help you focus. Answer these now as if money was not an issue and neither was time.

Thinking-Cap Time!

1. What do you feel most happy doing? What lights you up in life?

_____

_____

---

2 "Purpose," Dictionary.com, *Dictionary.com Unabridged*, Random House, Inc., http://dictionary.reference.com/browse/purpose (accessed: October 31, 2013).

2. If you could wake up tomorrow morning and be anything or do anything, what would it be?

_____

_____

3. When you find yourself in a joyful frame of mind, what are you doing?

_____

_____

4. What could you see yourself doing for the next thirty years of your life?

_____

_____

5. What are your most sincere values and beliefs?

_____

_____

Let's get some examples of answers from your peers:

- "I want to be someone that anyone can always count on."—Hero, 26
- "I want to know that I made a difference for sure. And I want to build up people to have that same passion as I do. There are so many younger people that don't have a desire to go very far, but a lot of younger individuals do have that drive and I want empower them."—Kara, 24

- "As a person that went out of their way to help others know God."—Mallory, 18

Little do you know, but these questions above are the foundation of your life. The choices we make as young adults affect our lives greatly in the future. Now, I'm not saying to always focus on the future and live in the future. What I am urging you to do is discover why you were created. There is a special reason, a specific reason. These questions will steer you in the right direction toward discovery.

Finding Your Purpose

This is the part where you dig deep inside the truest part of yourself. You will know it is your purpose if you have a deep emotion that clings to it. If it stirs something inside of you that you have never felt before, maybe you will dance around in excitement because you know, or maybe you will cry tears of joy for finding out, or maybe you will cry because you know you haven't been living your life from your truest desires. The answers to these questions will trigger something inside of you if you really quiet your mind, settle down to the demands of life, and listen to what truly makes you fulfilled.

If you find that you feel a little stuck on finding your purpose or your passion for life, here is what your peers are feeling and what they suggest:

- "You're not taking enough opportunities. You're not saying yes enough. You may be playing on Facebook too much or too much video games. Say yes to more opportunities."—Maeghan, 24

- "Find somebody that you would identify as a mentor, that you would reach out to and ask for a cup of coffee and say, 'I want to figure out what I want to do, how can I find that?' A lot of people have been there before and sometimes we just need a little help."—Kara, 24
- "I would tell them to stop looking. Just let it come. Relax, take a step back, evaluate, and enjoy your life and look from that angle, find that and harness that."—Hero, 26

It's okay not to know or to have some struggle with it. Try not to think of it as something you are trying to find, but rather as something that is already inside of you that you just have to connect with.

Once you have a pretty clear idea about what you believe your purpose is, start to make every decision you face based on the answers that you discovered in the questions above. If you are faced with a career choice, or a choice to go out with a friend, or a choice to judge someone, ask yourself, "Am I living from my purpose making this choice?" Go back to the answers to your questions and you will soon discover whether the decision you're about to make is the right one for you.

Let me give you an example. It was earlier this year where I really started to master the art of meditation. I was dealing with anxiety and some chronic worry in my life, and I felt as if the way for me to stay connected to my purpose was to meditate. I loved it. I felt so free afterward. My mind would drift and for twenty minutes of my day, I would forget all of my worries and problems and live in a state of knowing and empowerment. I also kept affirmations everywhere, on the walls of my room and in my car. I used words or sayings that would encourage me throughout the day to continue to live from my purpose.

I remember one morning feeling very anxious because I woke up late and was going to be late for work. So I quickly threw on some clothes and brushed my teeth. Well, I have a sticky note on my bathroom mirror that says, "When I am anxious, I will meditate, no matter what, I will go back 'home'." So I read that and thought to myself, "I'm late, I can't." I was just making excuses. So I got to work, sat down, and kept thinking about that note again, and I asked myself, *Am I living for my purpose, being anxious?* The answer was no, so I asked the girls in my office if they minded if I meditated. One of my coworkers suggested that we all do it. I couldn't believe it! So we shut off the lights, got on the ground, and listened to a CD that I used for meditation.

This was an incredible experience for me. The stillness in that room that day made me feel so centered with who I was, all because I had stepped out of the fear of what others would think of me and followed what I know my purpose is: to be anxiety-free and peaceful within myself. The feeling of what it is like to live from a place of peace is indescribable, and if we let ourselves step through fear and follow our dreams, anything is possible.

This was a small yet impactful moment in my life. When we live our lives on purpose, we forget about what others think. We are consistently in a state of gratitude, joyfulness, peace, kindness, and love. Ask yourself on a consistent basis throughout the day, am I living my purpose? Am I living *on* purpose? If the answer is no, quickly shift into what you know your heart is calling you to do. Watch how radically your life changes.

Chapter 6

Let the Haters Hate

Most haters are stuck in a poisonous mental prison of jealousy and self-doubt that blinds them to their own potentiality.
—Steve Maraboil

I love this quote by Steve Maraboil simply because it is so relevant to this chapter. All of us who hate on other people are just blinded by the potential that we all have inside ourselves.

Let's be honest: we've all experienced "hating" someone for what they have, what they've accomplished, even what they look like. We've all been walking down the hall or street or been at a party and seen someone walk by with a pretty blouse on, or nice jeans, or an expensive watch, or beautiful hair, and we've turned our noses up and maybe muttered or thought to ourselves something not so nice. It's human nature to want what others have, but it is one of the most damaging things we can do to ourselves.

Jealousy kills the soul's dream, and so does comparison. There is nothing worse than when we compare ourselves to other people.

We could not be further from our purpose. It's important to realize what effect this has on our lives. The more we get mad at others for what they have, the further away we are pushing ourselves from what *we* want. You might think, "That's not fair" or "They get everything handed to them." These are disempowering thoughts that aren't fair to us and to others.

The solution: be happy for the people who have something you may want. Yes, I said it, be happy. Whether it is a career, a car, a house, a body, a piece of clothing—be happy. Smile and say, "Good for them!" Because the same joy that they feel for having what you want will be transferred to you. We will never get what we want in life if we don't start to be happy for the people who already do.

The other side of this coin is that people will do the same thing to us. Once we launch and begin achieving our purpose, people will want what we have, but they won't know how to get it. So some will hate on us and be envious for what we have. So what do we need to do in return? *Show compassion*, because we were once in their shoes. Again, we need to show compassion for the people who say awful things to us because of what we've been blessed with.

Here's some wisdom: if we could *relate* to what another person may be feeling, then it would be very hard for us to ever judge again. What do I mean by relating? I mean that if someone is going through something that we once experienced, we can understand where he or she is coming from. If we don't, we need to show empathy and compassion. At one point in time, we were there. We were the ones hating on what *they* had.

How do we show compassion? *We help them.* We offer our love and help, but only if it is something they truly want. Some people won't want your help; they will be angry and bitter no matter what you do. If you cannot help them, that is when you walk away. Don't rub it in their face or show pride, *simply walk away.* This may be one of the most difficult things in life to do. One of my absolute favorite authors, Dr. Wayne Dyer, continually speaks about the idea that one of the three hardest things to do in life is to send love in response to hate.

I don't know about you, but this is truly one of the hardest things for me to do, even after practicing it a lot. To be able to love those people who treat you poorly, who look down on you, who say mean things to you. To politely send love and walk away is nearly impossible. But if we take that step, that step to choose kindness over anger and revenge, we free ourselves of the bondage and pain we will later feel. And let me tell you this: they are not going to know what hit them! They will have no clue how to respond or what to do, because it takes the wind right out of their sails. At that moment, your silence will have spoken volumes more than any words you could've said.

Learning from Those Who Disappoint You

Let me give you an example, from my own experience, of how hard it can be at times.

The college I'm attending is online with a nontraditional type of learning style. You actually get to pick your professors. There is a forum online where you post what you want to study in a particular field. For example, my field is psychology, so I would get to pick the topics I wanted to study and what professor was qualified to supervise my study.

The topic I wanted to study for that particular semester was spirituality, and I was researching the question, "What does it take for an individual to feel a sense of worthiness and love, and what does it mean to be spiritually connected?" I was so excited about this study because it resonated with me, and I *knew* the research would enable me to help other people as I pursued my passion.

As I was searching for the right professor, I came across one who was a life coach, an author, and a speaker. Her ideas had been featured on many popular television shows. She was everything I wanted to become! I was so ecstatic, I was jumping around my house for an hour. I was so elated ... until I reached out to her.

I sent her an e-mail that I put my entire heart into. I shared my passion with her, my deepest desires, all in one e-mail—and she never answered me! I spilled my guts out about my dream, vision, and passion, and she never even acknowledged my e-mail!

It really bothered. I kept thinking about it and reminiscing to whoever I could about what she had done. My mentor said that I probably intimidated her. And my gut reaction was, "Why on earth would someone like her be intimidated by someone like me?" She was so successful and had achieved things I could only dream of! I just didn't understand why someone would not offer any help or anything, especially after knowing how badly I wanted to work with her (at least how much I *thought* I did).

It truly crushed me until I stopped and thought about it. This truly was a learning experience for me and the reason I decided to write this chapter. I had to stop and ask myself, "What did I learn from this?" Was I mad? Absolutely, but I had to show compassion and realize I'd been there. I had to show her appreciation anyway, because deep down I knew that that is what I had to do.

Needless to say, I ended up not working with her and got an incredible professor who shared the same excitement as I did about the subject and offered me way more help than the other professor ever could have. I also walked away with a sense of peace for not letting my disappointment derail me.

It's okay to be different. It's okay to stand out, and it's okay to be unique. Ultimately, it's okay to be *you*. Celebrate your uniqueness. You are the only *you* on this planet. Don't listen to the people who put you down or discount you in any way, like this professor who didn't even have the courtesy to respond to my e-mails. Frankly, it doesn't matter what other people think of you. They don't know you.

You have permission to live out the life you have always wanted, simply because you breathe. Let the haters hate. Be mature enough to show compassion, relate to people, and send love in response to hate. Your haters may surprise you and start to become friends who you help to be successful too.

Thinking-Cap Time!

1. Who is the one person in your life you can start treating with kindness? Is it a parent? A friend? Make a commitment right now to change the way you have been treating that person. Accept him or her instead of judging. If you can do that, you can do anything.

_____

_____

2. How have you responded in the past to negativity? Is it similar to Mallory, age eighteen, who wrote, "For the people that didn't matter to me, I would just brush it off. But the people that do matter to me, it's harder to deflect negativity because it's from people you love."

_____

_____

3. What are three things are you committed to changing in how you treat people and/or how you respond to hatred?

_____

_____

The real lesson here is that it's so important to treat other people with kindness. We really truly have to respect and love other people. Sometimes all we really want is to be accepted by others just the way that we are, so let's treat others with the same mind-set.

The reality is that not everyone is going to like us and not everyone is going to treat us the way we should be treated, but it starts with ourselves. We must be the example first. You have no idea how much even a smile could mean to someone, or a kind word, or a compliment. You have absolutely no idea if that person really needed to hear it.

Let's start to get happy for other people and build them up. We're on a team, remember? So when someone on our team wins the game, it means we all win the game.

Chapter 7

Ladies First

To all my beautiful young ladies all over the world, this one is for you. From every woman with an aching heart to every woman in love, this is for you.

What if I told you that your only mission in life is to be happy? Someone once told me that my life purpose as a woman was just to be happy. I didn't know how to feel about that. I thought things like, *Well, how can I actually be happy?*

So I did my research. I read books and articles on women and love, and what has to happen in order for me to be "happy" or to live up to what women were originally created to be. As I embarked on the journey of meaning, connection, and a sense of worthiness as a woman, it began to lead me down roads I had never known. I became obsessed with what a woman's heart cry is, and what has to happen in order for us to feel fulfilled and be able to be in a loving, committed, deeply fulfilling relationship.

What I found was that we as women want way more than to just be happy. Of course, we want to be happy and want authentic happiness in our lives. Beyond that, though, the question that came to me was, "How can I feel a sense of worthiness and know that I am enough?" I began to discover through my readings and the experiences I had within me that what women truly want, deep down to their core, is to be enough and be accepted just as they are. Once we finally feel that we truly are enough in every sense of the word, *then* we can open our hearts to the love and vulnerability that we are so truly terrified of.

Here is what I know about *us*. We love to love. We're women. That is what we do best, that is why God made us mothers and why we are the nurturers. We love to care for others, we love to give, we love to be joyful, we love to dance, we love to laugh, we love to be free and feminine, and ultimately we love to give love to other people. When we love, we are also giving the other person the choice to accept or deny our love. Ladies, I know that sometimes our hearts get broken and crushed, and it can be one of the worst feelings on earth. It feels even more painful when we're younger because we are still learning and growing into who we are.

I have also found that when we love so deeply that we get hurt unexpectedly, it can ruin us. We can literally feel that we don't want to go on. It's the worst pain we ever will feel—emotional rejection. In other words, unrequited love. We are hoping, wishing, searching for someone to come along and mend our broken hearts and bring us the love and acceptance we so long for. You see, when we open our hearts to the possibility of love, we are also opening our hearts to the possibility of heartbreak. But without ever truly stepping out and valuing ourselves and experiencing that type of love, we will never be able to deeply love another. And this is where women miss the boat. They think they have to be someone else, or act a certain way, or sleep with a guy to be worthy, and that couldn't be further from the truth.

We can sometimes lie to ourselves when it comes to love, but the best thing I've learned through my own experience and the material that I've read is always be yourself and stay true to yourself. If you do that, you will never go wrong. When we stay true to who we are and someone loves us for *that* reason, it is so much more fulfilling than if we were to pretend to be somebody else that we know we are not.

- "I don't think I can do some things, I am too young. I am not good enough."—Erynn, 13
- "I feel as if I have to be perfect in this world, and I can't make a mistake."
- "I am afraid of exposing who I really am. I think I am afraid to love myself."—Heather, 19

It's no secret we sometimes struggle when it comes to our self-image and the way we perceive ourselves. We sometimes have unrealistic expectations placed upon our lives, and it is a lot of unnecessary pressure.

Just the other day, I was leaving my sister's house and tears began to roll down my cheeks because she doesn't think that her beauty and presence is enough. She began telling me how she felt that she had to prove herself through her work and redeem herself because she didn't feel *enough*. This is why I cried. My heart ached for her, because for so long I have had a burning desire to teach people (especially women) how to love and respect themselves, whether it is by exercising, eating healthy, getting out of a broken relationship, reading, organizing their life, having more joy in their life, switching their peer group, or living in the moment.

I long to help others through an act of kindness. It is and always will be about loving ourselves first. And here I was, listening to my sister who I would do anything for—yet I couldn't go inside her mind and change her perspective on how she felt about herself. My own sister!

What Are You Afraid Of?

Just couple of weeks after that, I woke up out of a deep sleep. It was like God had awakened me for a reason I didn't yet realize. I was wide awake, listening to the stillness of silence and the beauty of the quietness. My mind was racing with ideas and thoughts about this chapter. I remembered a conversation I had with a young adult who I know dearly, and I opened my notes.

I began to read, and these are some of the questions I felt led to ask: "As a young adult, what is your biggest fear about love? Think about it before you answer." And, "What excites you about love, if fear didn't exist?" Questions like these began to pour out of me at three in the morning. I also wanted to ask, "How do you know when you're loving yourself?"

When I asked this young adult the questions I'd been inspired to share, many answers came pouring out of her—answers like:

- "Getting hurt. I am afraid I will meet someone else and love him or her more."
- "I am afraid it won't last. I have *a lot* of fears."

- "I am afraid that the flame will eventually burn out. I sometimes believe that in the beginning it is all too good to be true."
- "I am afraid that person will get bored of me."
- "I am afraid to love myself."

Maybe you can relate to some of her fears? I know I can. We can overcome these fears, though, even if they are sometimes difficult to face. We can blast them, kill them, and destroy them so that we can be free to live the joyful, loving, fulfilling life we are called to live. I'll talk more about pressing and pushing through fear in chapter 14.

When I asked her, "How do you know when you love yourself?" she gave me an answer that was the very essence of this chapter:

You know you are loving yourself when you do what makes you happy. You know you love yourself when you take care of yourself. When you don't eat junk food, eat healthy, stay active … do hobbies you enjoy. That's what I need to do. I need to learn how to love myself more. I need to learn how to become my own best friend.

And I couldn't have said it better myself. How we treat ourselves, the thoughts we think, what we put into our bodies, and how we respond to people are all a reflection of how much we love ourselves. When someone says something bad about you, how do you respond? Do you respond badly back? Or do you send them love and walk away? When someone hurts you with their words, do you believe them? Or do you forget about what that person thinks of you? Are you doing the things you love to do? Are you making sure you block out more "me" time? Do you sometimes try to please everyone in your life because you're afraid of someone being mad at you and not liking you?

Everything in our lives that we are dealing with is a direct reflection of what we think and what we believe about ourselves. Horrible things may have happened to you in your past. I am not saying that it is your fault. I am simply saying that this day, this very day, we have an opportunity to change the way we feel about ourselves and what we will continue to accept in our lives and what we are not willing to accept.

All throughout our years of living and growing up, we experience pain, whether we like it or not. We experience people who tell us we can't do certain things, that we're not smart enough or that we will never make our dreams come true. Over this time, our love and passion for life dwindles. In order to get it back, we have to rewire our brain, if you will, and affirm ourselves. We have to give ourselves pep talks and dig deep within for the courage and strength to love ourselves.

If we feel sad or lonely about the relationship we don't have, or if we find ourselves not feeling joy or peace because we don't have a boyfriend or a girlfriend, we need to do the same activities with ourselves as we would do with another person. It goes back to loving ourselves first. We have to be that boyfriend or girlfriend to ourselves. We need to date ourselves! Go see that movie you want to see, wear that pretty outfit you would if you were going on a date, go out to dinner with friends, read a great book, call someone who makes you feel better, or simply write about how you are feeling in a journal. We have to stop waiting around for someone to sweep us off our feet. We need to be the woman someone *wants* to sweep off her feet.

I remember sitting on my couch one day, feeling very sad, overwhelmed, anxious, annoyed, pissed off, you name it, that was me. I was very stressed out because of everything I was doing: working full-time (even more), going to school full-time, and figuring out how I could achieve the dreams that had been constantly on my mind. I was thinking and thinking and thinking, and the more I thought, the more I became confused.

Finally I jumped up and yelled, "*Stop thinking, start doing!*" In that moment, I said, "Hailey get up—start taking care of yourself!" I threw on my tennis shoes and went to the gym, and I ran on that treadmill longer than I ever have. I ran for almost two hours! And believe me, I was not a runner. I took all my emotions out on that treadmill, and I couldn't have felt any better.

Afterward, I felt as if I could conquer the whole world. I could see clearly again. I felt inspired to love myself and do what I really wanted. In the times of the most pain, trust that you have the power within you to feel joyful, contentment, and *love* again.

Thinking-Cap Time!

Here are some simple questions to exercise your brains and help you make healthy choices and move in the direction of freedom. I would encourage you to think deeply and honestly.

1. Write down three fears you may have about love—it could be about yourself or a relationship.

    _____

    _____

    _____

2. What is it that you love to do? What makes you feel joyful? List the top three things.

    _____

    _____

    _____

3. What are three action steps you can take within *you* to love yourself more? (Examples: change eating habits, spend more time alone, read more, write more, and play more sports, spend time with friends.)

    _____

    _____

    _____

Love is the antidote to everything in life.
Without it in our lives and within our hearts,
our world will be meaningless.

Love and Acceptance

One of my favorite books, *Lovingkindness* by Sharon Salzberg, suggests something so insightful that I want to share it with you:

> We must move from trying to control the uncontrollable cycles of pleasure and pain, and instead learn how
> to connect,
> to be open, and
> to love no matter what is happening."[3]

---

3 Sharon Salzberg, *Lovingkindness* (Boston: Shambhala Publications, 1995).

This is written truth. What do you think was able to allow me to forgive my stepfather growing up? Love did—an undeniable love and acceptance for the person he was deep down. I'm guessing that he had to deal with plenty of troubles as a child too. I am sure he also felt alone and unloved at times, which may have led him to feel fear, guilt, and hatred. I forgave, one of the hardest things I think I ever had to do. But I knew in my heart if I was going to fulfill my mission and purpose, I had to love. And it takes authentic love to forgive another.

This is the same type of love that I ask us women to treat ourselves with: the love that has the power to forgive someone who has done something awful to us. It's the kind of love it takes for someone to look another in the eye and say, "I accept you with all of your strengths and all of your weaknesses." The love it takes to stand up for what we believe is right in our hearts and to never accept anything less than we deserve. The love it takes when everything seems to be working against you and you persevere anyhow. The love it takes to have our hearts shattered by someone we love and yet love that deep again.

This invisible yet powerful force in our world and inside of us is at our fingertips to do with whatever it is we want. *This* love I am speaking about is nothing we can ever find in our outer world. We can never find it in money, in clothes, in status, in anything worldly, only inside of ourselves.

Whenever I start to feel overwhelmed or a little bit of anxiety, I notice my breath. I place my hand over my heart and feel my breath and recognize this very moment is all I have. That to me is love. The breath inside of us is love. Our hearts are love. When we can slow ourselves down in a world that demands so much from us and recognize *love* we can see just how precious we are.

You will find this beauty when you know you are enough. You were made to do something great. You are beautiful simply because you breathe. The world needs your love, needs your desires, needs your presence and needs your gifts. Never forget who you are and where you came from. You came from pure, innocent, breathtaking love.

Chapter 8

The World Needs Millennial Men

G entlemen! You were made to be courageous. Growing up, sometimes you may have been told it is not manly to cry. But the word *gentlemen* broken up is "gentle men." Although we need your strength, courage, and drive, we also need your gentleness and kindness. You may feel as if all you're supposed to be is tough, strong, and successful, someone who make lots of money and supports a family. Although all of this is true, it misses the essence of what men really need in their lives. Don't worry; I'm not going to get all mushy on you here. Just stay with me.

You might be thinking, "What do you know?" Yes, I am a woman. But I'm not writing this chapter from a woman's point of view. I'm writing from a "human need" point of view. It is my belief that life itself should not have labels. Yes, men and women are different physically, but emotionally and spiritually we are all connected. There is a definite importance in what men are called to do in this lifetime, and I think it is crucial to examine where we are, where we would like to be, and what we can do to get there together. In order to feel connected, one must *be* connected—mentally, spiritually, and physically.

This is where a lot of my male interviewees helped contribute a deeper view from a male perspective at all the different ages of a millennial. I started to think about what would be important for you guys to hear and for you to know. I wanted to think of ways that you could be challenged and inspired, yet really gain some insight and value from this chapter. So most of the material in this chapter is from other men, in different age groups. No matter what your present age is, you can benefit from this chapter. Don't just take it from me, but from other guys who are millennials and are experiencing life with you.

Thinking-Cap Time!

A couple of different ideas came to my mind when I began thinking of questions I wanted to ask young men, and number one was about success. Success is very important to all of us, but it seems like there is an enormous pressure especially on men to succeed. Because of this pressure, some men define themselves by how successful they are, and when they're younger, it has importance in life over a lot of different things. Now, I can't see who is reading this book, so I cannot interview you, but I encourage you to fill out the answers to the same questions the other men did. This is more of an exercise for you gentlemen to see where your heads are at and to master this game of life.

My question to other millennials and to you:

1. How do you define success? Or more simply, how will you know when you are "in a good place" mentally, spiritually, and physically?

_____

_____

Since this chapter is specifically devoted to you, our gentlemen, I want to stress at this point that age is meaningless ... and yet not. You younger men do not have to wait until you are older to find your passion and direction. You can start by filling out your answers here with whatever comes to your mind to say. Success can be defined in many ways: how much money you have, what kind of job you get out of college, if you graduate *from* college, your relationships, it could really be anything. Success can also be recognized as achievement, if that is what you're more familiar with. Take a few moments and write down your answers, because this is going to be the platform for all the rest of the questions.

Here are some examples of how your millennial peers are defining success:

- "I define success as how many people are better off because you have lived."—Lonn, 25
- "Success to me is whether it is positive or negative in the world's eye. As long as I am doing the will of God then I am right where I need to be."—Jon, 28
- "I define success as getting good grades and my happiness."—Austin, 16

However you may define success, it is your success and no one else's. There is no right or wrong answer here. It is the first thing that pops into your head after you think of the question. Once you can see how your mind views success, then you can make the necessary decisions that will lead you on a path to achieve it. By the way, this changes as the years progress in your life, because each year, as you grow in maturity, your values and beliefs will also grow and then shape your perspective on success.

All right, still with me? I hope so. Next question!

2. What challenges or fears do you face as a man?

_____

_____

_____

_____

It's no lie that we all experience challenges and obstacles in our lives, but since I'm focusing this chapter on you as a man, I believe you would be surprised about how similar these challenges and obstacles are among men. I also believe there is a difference between a challenge and a fear. A challenge is a barrier or an obstacle that gets in the way—this could be a resource like money, time, and environment. Fear is something that completely stops you from moving forward from inside of you; no matter how much you want something to work out, you stay stuck.

And yet, you'd be surprised about how easily you can fix these fears and obstacles. It just takes a little bit of hope and a little bit of determination to move you forward in the right direction. Let's take a look into more hearts of men, as we explore what they say their challenges and fears are.

- "Not getting into college, and a fear of disappointing the people in my life."—Domenick, 13
- "At age twenty-five, I am afraid of turning thirty. Am I where I thought I would be at this age? My time clock is ticking."—Lonn, 25

These are all very valid and real fears and challenges. Do you have some of these same thoughts and worries? Take a deeper look at your answers to the questions above for a minute and ask if this is a challenge or a fear. Then ask, "Is my perspective realistic? And has my view of myself been stopping my growth as a man?" Once we are aware of our fears and setbacks, then we can start to learn, grow, and change.

As a man, I'm sure you probably feel the most fulfilled when you know you have succeeded and when you're contributing beyond just the simple mundane tasks of work and play every day. I can say firsthand that your strength and your willpower at times are inspiring. Sometimes women tend to be too cautious in their search for success. Successful men are those who can step up to the plate and become who they know they are created to be. You guys are meant to be happy and to live the life you have always wanted. Granted, success and goals are important, but what is even more important is the person you decide you want to be remembered as.

So my last question for you is:

3. What legacy do you want to leave in this world? In other words, how do you want people to remember you? Try to think of all the ways you want people to think of you.

_____

_____

_____

_____

You may have never even thought about this question before. But sometimes we fall into the trap of living in the moment—which is fine, to some degree. Still, we have to know what we're living for and why we are working so hard toward success.

Here are other answers from millennials about what legacy they want to leave behind:

- "I want to leave this world as a person who made others happy, who took people from point A to point B. They have better lives because I came into them."—Maeghan, 24
- "I want to know that I made a difference for sure. And I want to build up people to have that same passion as I do, to the individuals that have drive. I want to empower them."—Kara, 24
- "To be someone that someone can always count on. Dependable is the number-one important thing that I want people to remember me as."—Hero, 26

By figuring out what you want your legacy to be here on earth, you are setting up your life to live with purpose, and then you will "get somewhere!" You can always keep this in the back of your mind when making decisions. If they don't empower you to be better, stronger, more loving men, and if they are not a reflection of the legacy you want to leave, that choice may be the wrong one. It is always nice to have something to fall back on when you're stuck with making the right decision.

To be a leader in this generation, it's going to take guys who want to be men. Men make sure their choices in life match the legacy they want to leave. Men show respect for others and help other people reach success. Men know exactly what they want and do, and they do whatever it takes to get it—the ethical and moral way.

Find a Mentor

One of the things I would *highly* encourage you to do is to find a mentor. Find someone you trust and respect who is older and can guide you to the person you want to become. Pick someone who is a living example of who you would like to be. This is exactly what I am doing—surrounding myself with older, wiser, more experienced people so that I can learn things in a day that it's taken them years to find out.

Let me give an example of the value of a mentor. Years ago, I was approached at a networking event by a woman who wanted me to join her multilevel marketing company. We both had an extreme amount of enthusiasm and because of this, we connected right off the bat. I bought into every word she said to me. She began telling me how much money I could make and that I would be the absolute best and all that stuff. I was very flattered and very excited, and I may have been a little naïve ... you think?

I went home that night believing it was the best day ever, and I couldn't wait to tell everyone. Well, I decided not to say anything to anyone at first. I wanted a second meeting with this lady before I told everyone, because I kind of wanted it to be a surprise to prove how much of a big girl I was.

After we met the second time, this woman told me my investment would have to be well over $2,000 up front. Now, by this time I already trusted her and liked her, and she had showed me a plan for how I was going to make it back almost immediately. I was a little surprised by the price, but I still was going to sign the piece of paper because I never thought anyone would steer me in the wrong direction. However, something in me told me to wait to speak with my mentor.

I tried postponing the meeting and told the woman I would give her a call the next day. She was pushing me to call my bank and tell them to get the transaction started in the morning, which at the time would have pretty much cleaned out my whole bank account. It was late at night, but because my mentor and I were so close, I decided I couldn't wait for her advice. So I called right then and explained what was going on.

Well, my mentor flipped out! She was *so* glad I had called her because I was about to make a horrible decision. If someone was asking me to invest so much at the very beginning, it probably wasn't such a good idea. I was so thankful I had her to tell me this. She was older, she was more experienced, and she had my best interests at heart. It is at moments like that in my life when I feel so grateful to have a mentor.

From that day on, I have always encouraged friends and family members to get either a coach or a mentor. It really can change the direction and plans you have in your life, and you don't feel so alone in the decision-making process.

So men, I would strongly urge you to find a man that you admire and respect to be your mentor—someone who can help you navigate in this sometimes messy world. He will help you tremendously when it comes to what you want and how to be a successful leader in our world.

Be strong, courageous, intelligent men,
but don't forget to take your heart with you.

Chapter 9

Enjoy the Journey

Here is something you may not know about me this far into my book. One of the most challenging concepts for me to learn is how to have *balance*—to have fun and enjoy the journey of getting to where I am going. Sometimes I tend to be too serious and focus so much on my goals that I lose sight of my need for fun. Maybe some of you could help me? I am sure each and every person reading this book could help me in some way, just as I may be able to help you.

Here is the truth: I am still working on this part of my life, and I am discovering ways to have healthy fun in my life and celebrate my achievements each and every step of the way. Celebration of our achievements is one of the most important activities we could ever do in our lives. It is very important that we celebrate our greatest victories after we have worked hard to get where we're going. After we graduate high school, after we win an award, after we forgive someone, after we are kind to someone, after any act that took effort on our parts, we should celebrate.

We need to know the importance of not only celebrating our achievements but also celebrating who we are. In other words, celebrate our uniqueness. Each one of you reading this book has a unique gift to share with this world, and every single time you step through fear and become who you are and do what you love, you should celebrate.

Let me give you an example. I had a friend in high school who was very serious. She took everything so seriously and so literally. She was a straight A/B student and a leader in the choir, and almost every single teacher loved her. She excelled in everything she had ever done—she always was the best in sports—and yet she had no friends. Her weekends consisted of studying or practicing, either for singing or for her sport. She had absolutely no social life. She picked up a couple of part-time jobs to save money, so there was no time for school dances. And she barely got asked to prom.

Years after graduating from high school—she is now in her senior year of college—it is hard for her to make any friends. She is excelling in her professional life but has absolutely no idea how to have fun. As a result, she consistently struggles with relationships, at work, and in her personal life. She is working up to seventy hours a week, and she always appears to be *miserable* on the inside.

Now, why is that? She is someone who has everything at her age: she has success, she has status, and she has awards. But can you guess what is missing? Balance! She turned down every offer she received to have fun because she wanted to work. She longed for just a couple of close friends she could visit with throughout the week. Then she finally realized that her worth and importance weren't just about success, but about the relationships in her life that would make her feel fulfilled.

This someone was, and sometimes still is, *me*. I am the "friend." I may not be able to tell you how to have fun, or even really how to enjoy the journey, but what I can tell you is the affect it has on your life if you don't make it a priority to celebrate your achievements. When your life becomes all about succeeding and getting more and more, you lose sight of what is important. I am here to tell you that having fun in the process is a vital part of success. If you are anything like me—too ambitious and sometimes struggling with having fun—it is a very important part!

Healthy Fun

Most of our fun in this day and age consists of loud parties or wild crazy concerts that may include alcohol and illegal substances that aren't so great to be putting into our bodies. The choices you make in your life are none of my business, and I respect each and every one of us who makes those hard choices. However, I have been asked this question multiple times: "How do I have *healthy*, rewarding, exciting fun? Fun where I can remember doing what I was doing, fun where it lights others up and empowers my friends?"

So I am going to share a few ideas here that have really been working for me. Remember, I am still with you here; this is you and I together, growing and living *together*.

> 1. One of my coaches once told me, "Do something that you wouldn't find yourself normally doing on a daily basis." In other words, do something that is outside of your daily routine. This really resonated with me. It breaks the pattern of your everyday activities and makes your life more spontaneous. Some examples include going

to see a play downtown, going out to eat at a restaurant in a new town, seeing a movie, playing a new sport, going to a comedy club, or just simply hanging out and laughing with some old friends you haven't seen in a while, blasting loud music and dancing.

You could have a movie marathon with your friends, play cards, or just laugh! Laughing is so good for your soul. It is known to dramatically reduce stress and anxiety, and it naturally boosts your serotonin levels (the "feel good" chemical in your brain). The great news is that your body doesn't know if you're fake laughing or actually laughing, so "fake it till ya make it!" There are so many ways you can find to have fun!

2. Keep a journal. Write! This goes for guys too—it is not just a girly thing to keep a journal. One of the most profound things I have ever heard was, "When you are thinking thoughts and you don't know how to separate them, write them out." It really truly helps to collect your thoughts and to start writing. This may not be your idea of having fun, but writing down your achievements and celebrating them will help you remember them when you are at a low point in your life.

Whenever I feel afraid to do something or am in a situation where I really feel fear, I pull out my journal and read all of my achievements and triumphs, and I remind myself that I can do anything and that I am a success. If writing out your thoughts does nothing else, it helps you organize your beliefs and take back control of your life again. It helps to clear the mind so you can have fun.

3. Simply be creative. I think sometimes as young adults our creativity gets crippled—not because we aren't creative, but because our creativity can get crushed by

our stereotypes and by other people. We get so focused on succeeding and becoming something we think we are supposed to be. As we listen too much to the demands of the world, focus too much on college, or get sucked into drugs and alcohol to help alleviate our pain for a night, we can easily forget how creative we are.

We are born to be creative. Some of the best ideas that have revolutionized our country have been just tiny ideas that stemmed from creativity. Thinking "outside the box" sometimes involves taking new risks in an area you might not be familiar with. It challenges you to think deeper, tap into your own uniqueness, and discover your sincerest gifts.

Thinking-Cap Time!

Try this creativity exercise with me. Get out something to write on and draw a giant box in the center of a piece of paper. Make four boxes inside of the larger box. Now, let's start to think *outside* of the box. It will look something like this:

Write as many wishes as you have, i.e., become famous movie star, travel, discover a cure.	Write five ways you can help another person, i.e., a smile, a hug, writing a letter.
Write down objects you could make from a piece of paper, I.e., airplane, smiley face, paper ball.	Make wishes come true by, i.e., taking action, getting a coach, writing, setting goals and following through, believing in myself.

- **Top left box:** If a genie were to grant you as many wishes as your heart desired, what would your wishes be? Write those in this box.
- **Top right:** Write out five ways you could help another human being. This could be as simple as a smile. Remember, this is a creative exercise, so think *outside* of the box on this one.
- **Bottom left:** Think of all the different objects you can make out of a piece of paper, and write them out. Think of at least five things.
- **Bottom right:** How can you make your wishes come true?

If you would like to do it right here in this book, you can use this template.

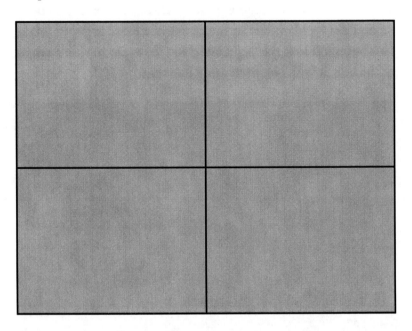

This exercise is a technique you can use on a daily basis. By writing out your deepest wishes, you begin to expand your mind to what is possible for your future. You see, you don't have to wish anymore when it is on paper. Though it may just be a dream in your mind, when you put it on paper, your dream becomes more realistic. With appropriate actions, your dream will start to materialize and become a reality. You will have new dreams as you grow, so continue to update this!

When you write in the second box about helping another person out, you start to view this world we live in as if we are all on one big team. What is the purpose of a team? If the Tigers only had a pitcher and not a first baseman, there would be no one there to catch the ball and the pitcher would have to work harder to make sure the runner got out. Our lives need to be about backing each other up and having each other's backs. We help each other out when others are in need, and the simplest way to do that is through an act of kindness.

Picture a girl named Sara from western Oregon who is a softball player. Right now, the bases are loaded. She hits the first home run she has had in her entire life of playing the sport. Just rounding first base, she tears a ligament in her knee and instantly falls, unable to run any further. The umpire warns the team that if they help her round the bases, it will be declared an out, and if she gets a substitute runner, her home run will be declared a single. After hearing this, two of her teammates came out on the field and walked her all around the bases. Her team backed her up when she needed it the most. Although the umpire ruled it as an out, it was still a homerun in her and her team's eyes because of their desire to help one another. (This is a true story.) [4]

That is what it means to be part of a team, when you stop thinking about yourself for one second and reach out and help another. There is true power in being kind to someone—a simple smile to the clerk while in line at a store, a simple hug when a friend needs it, giving someone your undivided attention, sticking up for someone when they are being treated poorly. I always make it a point when I am feeling down or discouraged to go and help someone else. It helps me realize the true reason we are here on earth. When we give to others, our entire life transforms into something great, into something worth living for.

---

[4] Sara Tucholsky, "Ultimate Sportsmanship." YouTube, May 5, 2008, http://www.youtube.com/watch?v=jocw-oD2pgo.

The box in the bottom left is there to disrupt your thinking. It's good to shift the mind every now and again. It enhances creativity. When we think of one thing for too long we get bored and stuck, which is no place we want to be. You can always change this up if you like. Maybe it's thinking of all the words that rhyme with *paper*. Anything at all to distract your mind for a little. This will open up avenues in the brain and will create another pathway for ideas.

The last box, the box at the bottom right, might be the most important. These are the steps we take in order to make the items in the first box a reality. It might seem far away, but it really isn't. The choices we make today dramatically affect our lives down the road, so even making the smallest changes in your life right now will enable you to move forward every day and take more steps toward your desires. Wishes will remain wishes without action. We must take daily action toward our dreams.

We don't realize it, but *fun* stems from creativity. Every thought, every idea, every desire of ours can become a reality with just a little bit of creativity. You want to be successful and have fun doing it? Be creative, be open to everything, be flexible in your thinking, and never forget to enjoy the journey.

Chapter 10

Become Successful *Your* Way, with or without College

Ever seen the poster with the phrase, "I want you to stay in school?" I think they showed this to me in high school a couple of times, and it's the first thing that popped into my head when I sat down to write this chapter. I hope you laughed a little bit. I still hear this all the time from my parents and grandparents. "Stay in school—I don't care what you do, just get that degree!" Have you heard similar statements? Maybe that is why you are in college right now.

This chapter will never answer the question, "Is college for you?" No one besides *you* can tell you if college is right for you or if it isn't. After reading this chapter, though, you will gain some insight as to how you can be successful in your own way instead of being influenced by friends or society. Now before you hurry on and flip to the next chapter, read a tad bit more.

Here are some statistics for you:

- **5.6 years**: Average amount of time it takes people to complete a bachelor's degree. It takes 4.4 years to complete an associate's degree.
- **19.7 million**: The projected number of students enrolled in the nation's colleges and universities this fall (year 2013).
- **$24,000**: The average loan debt per college student.[5]

I don't want this to sound like I am against students going to college by any means. For Pete's sake, I am still in college myself and about to graduate. I am simply stating facts so that you can make the best decision possible for *you*. Believe me, I understand the importance of school. My main message in this chapter is that you should become successful *your* way and understand what success means to you. It is different for each individual.

College is a very normal thing, and sometimes millennials are used to just going with the flow from high school and attending college simply because "it's what everyone else does" or "my parents are making me go." I would strongly encourage all of us to really think about the time and money we are investing in college and to really make sure that it is the path we are supposed to be taking. There are some occupations that you really have to attend college for—doctors, lawyers, therapists, for example. If that is *your* passion, I say go for it!

---

5 "Statistics about College Students," Stage of Life, accessed September 16, 2013, http://www.stageoflife.com/StageCollege/OtherResources/Statistics_about_College_Students.aspx.

Here are some opinions about the importance of college that other millennials shared with me—why they went to college or if they planned to, how it helped, and/or how it didn't:

- "School is good, but without experience I didn't know how to apply it. Knowledge is good, but I wasn't able to apply any of it. For example, economics—I don't care about that and I will never use it, so I would have to say yes and no."—Kara, 24
- "I went because my mom went. That's why I went to the school I went to. I knew that I needed it to get the jobs that I wanted."—Maeghan, 24
- "College was great, but I think that I got more out of my internship experience. Being around older generations has fined-tuned my skill set and taught me how to act appropriately in the workplace."
- "In my family it was expected. It was what you did after high school."
- "It wasn't until my senior year in college that I understood why I was going."

I have also heard comments like, "College was exactly what I needed to pursue my dreams" by other peers. It's different for everyone; my only hope for you is to make sure you're doing it for *your* reasons and no one else's.

It's also important to recognize and define what success means to us. Maybe for you it *is* getting a bachelor's degree or starting your own business. Or maybe you define success based on the quality of the relationships in your life. Anything in your life can determine how you define success.

Throughout my interviewing process, one of the questions I asked every time was, "How do you define success?" Now, remember, I interviewed millennials from all different age groups, from thirteen years of age to thirty-three. For Maeghan, age twenty-four, the answer was:

> I believe it is a feeling. It's not a destination, it's when you feel you are doing the absolute best for yourself and for those around you.

For others, the definition could be completely different. Lonn said:

> I define success as how many people are better off because I have lived.

In his case, success is measured based on how others are affected by his presence. This is a very clear answer on what he wants his legacy to say to the world.

Defining Success

The examples above show that each one of us really defines success in a different way. So I want to ask you the same question. How do you define success?

_____

_____

_____

It is extremely important to know how you define success because that is what you're going to be working toward your whole life. It is what makes you achieve your goals and what you work for every day. For the most part, this is what wakes you up in the morning; this is a portion of how we define yourself.

Everyone wants to succeed in this lifetime on some level, so if we know what drives us, then we can work toward that with enthusiasm. When you feel like you are succeeding and making progress in this world, you are one happy camper. On the other hand, when you feel as if you are just making it through another day, it can be discouraging.

As you consider what makes you feel successful, I want you to realize that all material things will pass. What I mean by that is if you believe that making a specific amount of money determines your success, you need to realize that all things that are of this world will eventually pass away. However, family, relationships, and love can also be a measurement of success. So let us not misconstrue success. It's not always about wanting more or getting more status or money or friends. It's about what we can give away to others, because the more we have, the more we should give away.

Remember when I talked about connection in the previous chapters? We can't forget how important connection is when we're identifying who we are and what's important, in addition to all the usual "worldly" goals. I once heard a statement that said achieving true success is when you help others become successful—that's true connection. In other words, when we are really successful, our mind-set changes from "How can I get more?" to "How can I give more?"

However you define success, it isn't right nor wrong. It is simply the way you view the world and your place in the world. It's okay if you want to define success based on how much money you are making, but understand that the relationships we build in order to share the things that we get—the connections we make—are always important in our lives.

Evaluating Your Values

Here is a more step-by-step process for discovering what motivates you on a daily basis. Start by writing out your top three values in life:

_____

_____

_____

Values can be defined as things of relative worth or importance. In other words, these are the things that are most important to you in your life—the unconscious and conscious motives you use to make your daily decisions. Your whole decision-making process is based upon these values.

When asked about values, Jon defined his as "faith, integrity/ character, and family. Every decision Jon makes is going to be based on his faith, his integrity as a person, and the impact on his family. With even the smallest example—choosing to eat an apple over a cookie—he might think of his family or his character in terms of his health, and he might want to make a better decision based on what he values in his life.

For Austin, the important values were "school, hockey, and freedom." Judging from his values, Austin may make choices based on how they will affect him in school or hockey. These are the reasons he makes one choice over the other. He'll go to hockey instead of watching a movie at night, or if he does both, hockey is going to come first.

Jot down your own top three values and keep a close eye on them. They may change, and so may the reasons behind your choices about school or work or both, or your choice about marriage, having children, or going out for a sport. This part of your life is about *you*. It is your time to think about yourself and what the standards are for your life.

So now we have two sets of answers: how you define success and what your top values are. What do we do now? Did I just hear you say, "Let's evaluate?" Great! This is the evaluation part. This is determining whether or not we like our answers and/or if it's time to make a change.

Now, you may be very happy with your values and your area of success, which is awesome! That's where I want you to be. But if you're feeling like other influences have had an impact on your decisions and choices lately, we should reevaluate those values.

The quickest way to know if your values are helping or hindering you is to examine your life. Are you cheerful on a daily basis? Do you feel like you help others? Do you feel like you're making a difference? How do others respond to you? You can get the answers to these questions very quickly with a short examination of your life and where you are today.

It is easy to get caught up in a world where people control what you think, what you believe, and what you do. Always, always,

always go back to your values and what is significant to you, regardless of what anyone else says or thinks. Keeping what you stand for at the forefront of your brain will help you maintain confidence in your decisions and design the life that you want for yourself.

> *The major value in life is not what you get.*
> *The major value in life is what you become.*
> —Jim Rohn

Chapter 11

The Power of a Mind-Set

What if I told you that you are only as young as you *think* you are? Or as old as you *think* you are? What would you say to that? Would you believe me? Or would you completely think I was crazy? Well, I am here to tell you that your mind is one of the most powerful tools you will ever have. And the great thing about that is you never have to lose it! Once you realize the power of your mind, you have opened your life to anything you have ever wanted to do. Any dream, any desire, any hope—anything can be yours with the right mind-set.

It is said that we have over sixty thousand thoughts a *day*. Can you believe that? We cannot consciously comprehend controlling all of our thoughts, but what if I told you that you could? If you take anything from this chapter, make it this: what you think about will be the product of your life. What I mean by that is what you consistently think about on a daily basis shapes your decisions and therefore your future. You may be thinking, "Well, I don't know what I think about," or "I have no idea how to control my thoughts." What I can tell you is that even though it is not easy, it is essential to understand that how you think of the world and yourself is what determines your success or failure.

For example, have you ever been speeding down a road because you were in a major hurry, running late, and you consistently hit every red light, or that person who got in front of you was going ten miles per hour under the speed limit? None of that was by accident. If you stopped and asked yourself, "What am I thinking?" it's usually thoughts of worry and anxiety about being late. This happens to me all the time, and once I realized my thoughts were the problem, I started to shift my mind into thinking, "I am fine, I have plenty of time, I will get there. You're fine, Hailey." Things started to change dramatically.

Don't believe me? One night when I was driving down a highway, I had two paths I could take to get home. I was running late and had to stop at home and change my clothes really fast. So I began to take some deep breaths and tell myself I had plenty of time. I decided to take the route on the right of the fork in the road instead of the left, even though I rarely went that way. As I looked to my left, I saw backed-up traffic, bumper to bumper, because there had been an accident. You may call that a coincidence, but I believe that everything happens for a reason and there are no accidents. Two days later, the same thing happened to me again!

This is just a minor example of how our thoughts affect the way we live. If you start with something small like this, watch how it works. You will start to be more conscious of what you think about.

Let me give you another example. When I was working part-time as a waitress a couple of years ago, I made the most money on days when we were the deadest and so slow. Let me tell you why. On my way to work, before every single shift, I would say these words: "Abundance is coming my way today. This is going to be the best shift I've ever had." I would say this over and over and over again, but I also *believed* it. I believed that the words I spoke would have an effect on my night.

I would repeat those words during lineup before our shift started. Everyone laughed at me. I was fun to watch and somewhat entertaining. They snickered and thought I was crazy, but I was the one laughing all the way to the bank. Out of nowhere, large parties would sit in my section and would tip me close to 40 percent. I had the best customers and made some awesome connections with people. My tips nearly doubled in two weeks simply because I said those words. And this happened when we were supposedly in the slowest time of the year.

I've seen this change not only in my own life but in the lives of many other people. If your thoughts are consistently focused on what is wrong with your life and what you *don't* want, you will continue to get in return what you think about. But if your thoughts and words reflect a heart full of gratitude, love, kindness, and encouragement toward yourself, things will start to appear and happen in your life that you'd have never thought possible.

This chapter is all about the power of a mind-set. Age is meaningless and just a way for humans to measure time. Who you *think* you are is who you start to become. Every single morning I wake up and utter the words, "Thank you." Then I wait to see all that I have to be thankful for that day. It's the most amazing thing.

This isn't just positive thinking. This is a lifestyle—a lifestyle in which you choose to look on the bright side instead of the dark side, a lifestyle in which you start to think thoughts that are loving toward yourself and other people. We can create, destroy, build up, tear down, succeed, or fail, all with our minds.

Have you ever wondered why some people are really happy in life while others are miserable? Have you ever seen two people in the exact same situation and one is joyful while the other is unhappy and distraught? People don't just have bad luck or good luck. Granted, it is true that bad things happen to good people, just as good things happen to bad people. There exists the inevitable— things are going to just happen that we don't have control over. What I'm trying to tell you is that we create the lives we think we deserve for ourselves. By setting a new standard of what we are going to think about, we are setting a new standard for ourselves and our lives.

Change Your Words, Change Your Life

Think about how we hear people say all the time:

- "Oh, me! I am just too old."
- "I am getting so old."
- "I am way too young for that."
- "I don't have enough life experience."
- "I have to prove myself to other people once they see how young I am."

All of these thoughts are damaging and ridiculous! They are complete and utter lies that we tell ourselves in order to stay stagnant in our lives. Here is an example from Kara, age twenty-four, that maybe you can relate to:

I had a senior executive that I was meeting with, and he said he had five kids, and "my oldest daughter is twenty-six, yeah, probably your age ..." He trusted me and had confidence in me over the phone, then once he saw how young I was, he had changed his credibility for me once we met face to face.

It is no wonder we may feel like our age has such a big thing to do with it. I know I always feel like I have to prove myself to other people because of how young I look. I have had people completely ignore everything I said simply because I lacked experience. I know life experience is important, but it is not everything.

Start believing that you matter! Your opinion, no matter what your age, matters. You have a voice and no matter what stage of life you may be in, *it matters*. You have something to share with others that they don't have. Everyone needs to hear what you have to say. It *is* important to others, and the only way you're going to have the confidence to speak up is to first have confidence in what you think about yourself and the world around you. You can simply start by saying:

"What I have to say matters, and I won't hold back anymore."

Here's another encouragement for you:

- Instead of thinking, "I can't wait for this day to be over," "I hate Mondays," "This weather is so crappy out," "I can't stand my life," "I am so annoyed," or "I am so tired," replace those thoughts with, "I wonder what great thing is going to come out of today?" "This is the only day that I have; I am going to make the best of it," or "My life is what I make it; I choose right now to be happy."

One my favorite authors, Louise L. Hay, wrote a book called *Power Thoughts: 365 Daily Affirmations* that gives you an affirmation a day for a year, something to think about and help shape the direction of your mind. I would strongly encourage you to get a copy and retrain your mind each day of the year with thoughts of empowerment and love.

When we were younger, we were not programmed to think positively about the world. In fact, we were always told, "No, don't touch this," or "No, don't do that." Some of us were taught that we can't trust anyone, and we always needed to work really hard to get anything, and life is a struggle. We weren't raised to think optimistically or to look on the bright side. As we get older, our society and the people in our lives impact our thinking with their own thoughts.

Start with even a small change in the way that you speak and watch how drastically your life changes. People will start responding to you better and more opportunities for success will come your way. You will make connections that will catapult you to a higher level in your career. Your overall health will improve and you will have more energy to do the things you really want to do. You won't feel so tired anymore.

Some of us are just plain old exhausted! Are you with me? I hope you're still following. Sometimes we are just so tired. Tired of being someone we aren't, tired of the way our life is, tired of feeling bad, tired of getting nowhere in life, tired of other people judging us, hurting us, and letting us down. Tired of fear holding us back, tired of feeling guilty. We are *so* tired.

I believe the main reason most young adults are so emotionally tired is because we have built up walls in our minds that enable us to be less than what we really can be. We think that what we are going through right now is permanent, and sometimes we believe that we are stuck with what we're doing and that our life is already mapped out for us. This isn't true, but it starts to be our reality.

Og Mandino is an inspirational writer and has a gift of sharing an important message with the world through a powerful story. I mentioned in my introduction that I have read plenty of self-development books, and I have read all of his. In one of his best-sellers, *The Greatest Miracle in the World*, I stumbled upon this quote, and it truly impacted the way I think.

> You see, Mister Og, most of us build prisons for ourselves and after we occupy them for a period of time we become accustomed to their walls and accept the false premise that we are incarcerated for life. As soon as that belief takes hold of us we abandon hope of ever doing more with our lives and of ever giving our dreams a chance to be fulfilled. We become puppets and begin to suffer living deaths."[6]

This is so true in our lives! We at times build prisons in our minds and believe that when we think thoughts of discouragement, of fear, of bitterness, of doubt, of shame, of guilt, of hopelessness, of anxiety, and of stress that they are there to stay. And so, as Og wrote, we "suffer living deaths." Although we are alive, we are not living. We may be living lives that someone else has planned for us, or we are living our lives according to what everyone else thinks versus what our hearts are really urging us to do. We are too young to be doubting our worth and value; we are too old to be wasting another day not doing what we love.

---

6 Og Mandino, *The Greatest Miracle in the World* (New York: Random House, 2009), 17.

It all starts with how and what we think about ourselves. It starts within our minds, which create our life. You want to change your life? You can right now by choosing to examine your thoughts and make them work *for* you rather than *against* you. My absolute favorite author, Dr. Wayne Dyer, consistently suggests that your thoughts create your reality. His book *Change Your Thoughts, Change Your Life* very much *did* change my life. In it he writes:

> Ask yourself right now, *What's my own nature if I have no outside forces telling me who or what I should be?* Then work at living one day in complete harmony with your own nature, ignoring pressures to be otherwise. If your inner nature is one of peace, love, and harmony as a musical genius, for instance, then act on just that today.[7]

I couldn't have said it better. When we listen to our own voice, our own thoughts, we can make a decision to follow our gut rather than the voice of someone else. What you consistently tell yourself in your mind becomes who you are. I believe everyone should read at least a portion of Dr. Dyer's work; he has dedicated his life to helping others, and you will realize too that our thoughts are the only thing holding us back from having whatever it is we crave in our lives.

Forgive and Live

Let me give you one final example of how changing your thoughts and the words you speak can dramatically change your life. When I met my biological father for the first time at age fifteen, he and I had a really rocky start. As you can imagine, it was two worlds

---

7 Dr. Wayne Dyer, *Change Your Thoughts, Change Your Life* (Carlsbad, CA: Hay House, Inc.), 63.

colliding as we tried to figure out what role each one of us would play in the other's life.

I was an extremely angry teenager. I was mad at the world and how I was being treated, so I would lash out at other people because that made me feel important. Meeting my real father and finding out we had only lived within fifteen minutes of each other my whole life made me even madder.

That's the situation he was walking into. He didn't yet know that I didn't need a disciplinarian but *love*. I craved love so much growing up, and that's ultimately what I needed the most. We both had no idea how to be in this relationship, and therefore it was crazy, to say the least, for the first couple of years.

I was so mad at my dad for not giving me what I needed. I felt abandoned; I thought that if he had been there, I wouldn't have felt this unconscious pressure to take care of my family. I was so angry that I wrote him a good-bye letter and didn't speak with him for over six months. I sought out a therapist to help me overcome my hurt and bitterness, and we started with my thoughts.

With the therapist, I started to examine what I had been thinking about and identifying myself as for the past several years of my life. She worked with me for years. I started to develop the patterns that I am writing about right now. I completely rewired my brain for what I ultimately needed to do, which was forgive and accept.

When I say my entire life changed after I forgave, I mean my *entire* life. I went to both of my fathers after almost a year of no communication and forgave them. I had to take ownership of everything that I said and did wrong. I had to accept that although my hurt was valid, it was no longer serving me. From that moment on, my life has never been the same.

Within one year I quit my job, started at Dale Carnegie Training, coached, and went through all of the training to be an instructor for the course. By the time I was nineteen, I had coached hundreds of people. And then, within one month of finishing my time at Dale Carnegie Training, I started writing this book you are reading now. I found a publisher and three editors for my book all within one week and found the funds in one day to pay for the production of my dream. Now I am on my way to pursuing my deepest dreams—all because of the power of forgiveness and my willingness to accept all people for where they are in their lives and not hold grudges for anything that has ever happened to me.

It really is the most exhilarating feeling in the world to let go of the control that anger has on your life and watch how much your life changes. For me, it made the difference between *fulfilling* my dreams and *crushing* my dreams. Let me tell you, it was one of the hardest things I've ever had to do, but it was the *only* thing I could do so that my life could go on.

Another great book that has helped me with acceptance is *Lovingkindness* by Sharon Salzberg. What she has to say about our minds and anger is so reflective. She writes:

> When our minds are full of anger and hatred toward others, in fact *we* are the ones who are actually suffering, caught in this mind state. But it is not so easy to access that place inside of us which can forgive, which can love. In some ways to be able to forgive, to let go, is a type

of dying. It is the ability to say, "I am not that person anymore, and you are not that person anymore."[8]

This is very true; we are dying to our old self that would hold onto things and make them worse. We are literally changing our perspective about the other person and about ourselves.

If there is someone you are angry toward or if you are holding onto something that you know isn't good for your life anymore, my hope is that you'll learn to forgive and show compassion to that person. He or she may be hurting too. Don't do it for anyone else other than yourself. Everything will start to line up for you in your life just like it did mine when you accept and forgive. It begins by first forgiving ourselves. Stop being so hard on yourself when you make a mistake or do something you wouldn't normally do. Just begin by saying,

"Everything I've said and done, and everything I haven't said or done, I forgive myself in this moment."

This all starts with what we think about. If you can't tell right away what is going on in your head, start by noticing the words you're saying. Do you speak life to other people? Words that will build them up? Or do you speak down to others? Words that will tear them down? Most importantly, what do you say to yourself?

---

[8] Sharon Salzberg, *Lovingkindness* (Boston: Shambhala Publications, Inc., 2008), 73.

Thinking-Cap Time!

Right now, let's write down one thought you are committed to start thinking daily. I'll go first: *Hailey, you are more than what others think about you.*

Now, your turn:

_____

_____

_____

If we start to review these every day, eventually we will start to create a life of fulfillment and true joy. Just remember, you can choose right now to make the decision to start believing anything is possible by simply *thinking* that it is.

Chapter 12

Evaluate Your Friendships

Friendship is such a beautiful gift in our lives. It's two people who completely accept one another's identity: who they are, what they do, what they say. They can act the way they want, without judgment. Friends know things about you that no one else can. Friends are there to build you up on your worst days and laugh with you on your best days. I have some friends I call just to hear their voices, because a simple hello can calm me down. Friendship plays a role in our lives we can never replace.

We were made to be social beings. Part of our survival as humans is the connections we have with other people. Remember that word *connection*? It keeps popping up! Coincidence? I don't think so. But to go on, we are not meant to hide out all day by ourselves. Building relationships and growing in friendships is an essential part of our lives.

With that being said, most of us are starved for good solid friendships. Nowadays, it can be hard to come by people who accept you unconditionally, who you can completely trust. So it can be easy to only look at the good qualities in your friends and ignore the parts that you know aren't good for you.

It's been said that the top five people you hang around with are ultimately who you end up being like. The only question I have for you is, do you like what you see when you look at your sphere of influence? Do you like what you are becoming, having the friends that you have? In other words, are your friends helping you become a better person? Are they helping you grow into the person you want to become? These are questions I always ask myself, which might be the reason why I have lost a lot of friends in the last couple of years. My bottom line has always been that if my friends are not helping me grow, then they have to go.

When friends are such an important part of our lives and we crave connection with people, we may excuse some "minor" issues and not recognize that their values may be different from ours. It always comes back to values. That's why it is so important to recognize what your core values are, so that you can match them to the type of people you want to be around. It's easy to excuse the things we don't like about our friends when we crave their companionship. But we have to be very careful, because they are who we start to become.

For example, I used to hang out with a certain group of people who liked to do things that I didn't so much agree with, and they liked to watch movies I wouldn't normally watch. I also had bad eating habits only when I was with these friends. I would eat junk and I would put things into my body that I knew deep down weren't good for me.

I started to think differently about myself. My friends were "fear-based," which means they operated and made decisions based on how it would look to other people and not what they knew was right. I started to do the same thing. I used to care so much about what others thought of me, and I know this because I was constantly saying "sorry," "oh sorry," for things I didn't have to be sorry for. I was always excusing myself for little mistakes and worrying about what the person I was with was thinking.

I was super self-conscious about myself and the way I looked. It completely controlled the way I lived my life, and it really had a lot to do with the people I hung around. I started to notice that my friends did the same thing.

Be careful, because it is easy to blame your friends for your problems, and you may even think that your friends are the ones causing the issues in your life, but you have to look at yourself first. One of the millennials I interviewed, Jon, age 28, said something so profound about the people that are in our lives: "People will come into your life, and they are a direct reflection of your heart's choice."

What I interpret him to be saying is, first comes us and then comes our friends. I do believe we get to choose our friends, but I also believe we choose our friends based on the heart and mind we use to pick them. What do I mean by that? I mean that first our hearts and our minds choose the kind of people we want to hang around with and then those people show up in our lives.

This is what happened to me because of my insecurities and worry about pleasing other people: I had friends who reflected similar fears. Once again, it goes back to our minds and what we think we deserve. I'm sure you've all heard the phrase "quality over quantity." Having a few good solid friendships can be better than simply having a bunch of people you call friends.

Once you are crystal clear on the values you have in your life, everything will start to fall into—or out of—place. It all has to do with what you believe to be true about yourself and about other people. For example, one of my top values is lifelong learning, so I love to surround myself with people who also have a hunger for knowledge and get as excited as I do about learning new things.

For me, it all comes back to growth. Do I feel like I am growing with this friend? Does he or she crave knowledge like I do, and do we help each other become better people? Happiness and joy are also values of mine, so do my friends love to laugh? Do we have healthy fun together? Do we create an atmosphere that makes other people feel included? These are questions I make sure I go back to, based upon my values.

So examine your values. You can go back to chapter 10 if you need to look at what you wrote earlier. See if what you value is true for your friends too, and see if what is most important to you in your life is important to them too. This is in no way, shape, or form judgment or criticism; it is simply evaluating your life in terms of who you choose to spend your time with. It is a very important step in creating your life. By choosing who you want to spend time with, you are also picking who you want to be in life.

Our friends have influence in our lives, and we also need to recognize that we are constantly influencing them. What we may forget is that we can have a major impression on the people we surround ourselves with.

My sister was on a mission trip with her friend, and they were huddled together talking. They had to share things that they liked about each other. This friend told my sister that if my sister wasn't so committed to the church, then this friend wouldn't have been as involved in the church either.

My sister had let this friend go in earlier years and distanced herself because my sister was growing and her friend's values didn't match hers. But my sister still had a major influence on her friend's life because of the example she was living, and that's the reason her friend eventually came around to go on this trip. My sister had been impacting her friend's life for years and didn't even know it.

Just as our friends have influence over our lives, we are constantly influencing the lives of the people *we* are around. Remember that people are watching us and that we influence others a lot more than we think. Are we setting positive examples for others to follow, or are we constantly struggling to make and keep great friends?

Your peer group may be one of the most important choices you make in your life, because it ultimately determines who you are. Never forget that you are always influencing people wherever you go and are setting examples for those who look up to you and those around you. We leave imprints wherever we go, but would we want to go back and see what we have cemented? You know how people cement their hands in their driveways and then go back and see the imprint. That's how we make imprints in people's lives. And they're there forever. What imprints are you making in the lives of the people you care about?

Chapter 13

Learn from the Past, Plan for the Future, Live in the Now

Learn from the Past

"**I**'m going to teach you a lesson!" When I was growing up, I heard this phrase over and over again in my household or in school. Have you ever heard this? Whether it is our parents, our guardians, or our teachers, people want to teach us something, and they want to make sure that we get the lesson.

I started to relate this to my life when I was younger, and even now I still do. I consistently asked myself, "What is there to be learned in this situation?" When I was faced with a struggle, I quickly discovered that instead of moaning, "*Why me?*" in my head I could change the question to "What can I gain from this experience?"—even if I was in what seemed to be a most horrible situation, from having no friends to the very few that I did encounter always putting down my dreams and telling me I was never good enough, or people saying that I was weird and didn't "fit in."

People would look at me as if I had just cussed in church when I would tell them I was writing a book. I had people mock me for my ambitions and vision and tell me I was completely crazy for believing I would ever amount to anything. Even in those tough situations, I had to ask myself, "What am I learning?" I learned that not everyone is going to have your back. I learned to be cautious about who I tell my most intimate desires to, and I learned how to really believe in myself when at times it felt as if no one else did.

You see, everything we go through can be a learning experience; everything can be considered a gift along the way. Whenever we find ourselves in a situation, whether it is a great experience or a daunting one, there is always something to be learned. Everything that we went through as kids or are still going through contains something we can learn from. You were and still are in the middle of one of life's greatest lessons.

I like to view my life as one big canvas, and I am the one holding the paintbrush. When we were younger, we were not the ones holding the paintbrush. It was our parents and guardians and others who were painting our picture. What did your picture look like? Did it look like a beautiful ocean with mountains in the distance or was it more of a dark night with a tornado going through it?

Whatever it may have looked like, there is something we can learn from those experiences. I can't tell you what you learned because I am not sure exactly what you have been through or what you may still be going through, but what I can share is that there have been many successful people who came from the worst places. If they can do it, you can too. There is nothing different about you and no reason you cannot be what you want to be.

*We sometimes fall into the trap of believing
that our past is what defines us.
We hold onto our past like we're rolling down a roller coaster
with our hands so tightly gripped on our past
that we forget to experience the rush of
going forward into our future.*

In this moment, right now, it is time to let go. Let go of the past hurts, struggles, pain, guilt, fear, worry, and turmoil. Let them go. Take one big breath in and breathe slowly out. You are letting go of everything that does not serve you any longer. It's a freeing feeling when you let go and learn from your past instead of tightly hanging onto it. You might have been holding onto something that wasn't ever there. Affirmations also are critical when you're trying to let go of your past.

Once we can understand the lesson our past could be teaching us, we can leave it behind. It is at that moment when we can plan for our future. This is my favorite part, because we only have one life, one chance, and I want to make it count. I don't want my past to dictate in my mind how I am to live my life.

How about you? Thinking about and planning our futures is one of the most exciting phases in our lives. This is the time when you can think *big*, think about anything you want to become. This is where anything is possible. You have the paintbrush in your hand and it is your canvas to paint. This is where you find out what exactly you want and then plan it.

Plan for the Future

This is where we are going to create our vision for ourselves. You are going to want to create something so compelling that you think about it nearly every day. This is that one thing that keeps you up at night. I can honestly say that the majority of my book has been written in the middle of the night, because my vision was so enthralling for me that I couldn't sleep.

I seriously think of my vision every day. I used to joke with my coach because I would have dreams while I was dreaming; I would dream about my dreams! That is how much I have fallen in love with my vision for myself—in other words, what I want my life to be full of. My vision is what I absolutely want to achieve in my lifetime, and it is going to impact the lives of people around me.

Sometimes it can be a little scary planning for the future and creating our vision. One of the questions I asked millennials was, "Does preparing for the future make you nervous?" I heard multiple responses. Maybe you can relate with some of their answers:

- "Absolutely 110 percent, because I feel like it is a constant racing of the clock."—Hero, 26
- "No, 'cause I don't prepare for anything. It might change, but not right now."—Mallory, 18
- "I fear the unexpected of what could happen. I don't know what to expect."—Mallory
- "Yes, 100 percent. Currently I am single and not knowing if I am going to have a family or where that part of my life is going. It makes me nervous because if I always have to support myself that is a lot of responsibility."—Kara, 24
- "In my organization I feel secure, but it's not all about my company. If something goes wrong with America, or my company, or what if I get sick and can't work, I won't make money."
- "The pressure to perform is very high for us."

Some of us don't want to even think of the future because of how nerve-wracking it can be. I can completely relate to these answers. We have these set standards in our society, and sometimes not being taken seriously in the workplace can damage our confidence in our abilities and lives.

I want to share some other answers I heard because I think it's important for us to look at some of the struggles we are facing as a generation so that we can work together to break down stereotypes. Here is what Kara, age 24 says,

- "We have pressure to succeed when we are successful because of the large amount of people who believe we are lazy and don't want to work."
- "We almost have two walls we have to tear down first, and then maybe, just maybe we can breathe. It's just not fair."
- "Juniors in college are feeling extra pressure to have real work experience and own their own businesses because how tough it is to find and keep a job."
- "I have to have proof that I'm good, before I even start, in order to be successful."
- "We are constantly trying to defend ourselves and prove ourselves that we have what it takes to be successful."

I wish I could take all of your thoughts too and put them into this book, because I know you may be experiencing the same kind of anxieties and frustrations when preparing for the future.

Although these fears are very real for us, we shouldn't let thoughts that reek of discouragement and/or self-doubt hold us back. Don't let the demands of others, negative comments, and society's stereotypes affect your attitude and what you put into your life.

We have to understand we live in a completely different era, and the other generations aren't the enemy. We just need to know how to be ourselves and what we consider effective in today's thriving time.

One of the things I do with my vision so that I can reinforce the success of my future is to literally visualize what my life could be. There is strong power when you envision your life exactly as you want it to happen. Envision it like you have already experienced the dream. When I close my eyes to envision something my heart truly desires, I picture myself being there, doing what I see, really truly experiencing it—as if it is a memory I am replaying in my head.

As an example, my friend called me about a month ago and was conflicted because she really wanted to move out of state to be with her friends, but she was having trouble finding a job. She told me how everyone around her was telling her that it would be impossible for her to find a job out of state because they don't hire people normally without them living in the area.

When she called me she was feeling pretty discouraged, because she was starting to second-guess what her heart was truly telling her to do. I said, "Sarah, you cannot listen to what other people say. You cannot listen to other people's discouragement when you know it is something you deeply want." I asked, "Do you want to move out there?"

She said, "Well, yeah, I mean, yeah, I want to."

So I said, "Now say, I *am* moving out there." And I made her say it a couple times. Lo and behold, not even a month later, she got a call from a friend and accepted an amazing job opportunity in a town she loved that was close to her friends.

That was no accident. She disregarded what others were saying and changed her words to "*I am*" versus "I want to." I told her to see herself there, packing, getting ready, quitting her job here, and doing all the other things she had to in order to make it happen. She was the one who ultimately did all the shifting inside herself and made it happen; I just helped her look at it in a new perspective.

Don't be afraid to think future, dream future, plan for the future, and envision your bright future with something that you *really* want! Stop seeing it as something you have to "go out and get." See it as something you already have. You just have to tap into that part of you that is connected to it already. A tiny shift in words can dramatically change the direction of your life.

Write the vision you have for your life here as if you are replaying a memory in your head—as if it is already has happened or is happening now.

_____

_____

_____

_____

_____

I have read about a couple of different things that you are supposed to do with your vision to make it more real. I've read that you could post it on your wall, in your car, or somewhere else where you can see it every day. I have also read that you could write it out, recite it once, and then put it away. What I would say to you is to do whatever your heart desires. I've done all these, but I am a big believer in affirmations and putting them somewhere where I will be constantly reminded of them. After some time, I won't need them up there and the thoughts will just come to my mind automatically. My suggestion is to find what works for you, but at least have a vision.

Live in the Now

We will never get this moment back, so cherish every second of it. I am sure you have heard something like this before, but it is true and something that I, myself, know I always forget. We can get so caught up in our future and our past that we forget today is a gift we will never open again. Getting our high-school diplomas, college graduation, birthdays, even a simple Sunday with the family—precious moments fill our lives all the time. Be in attendance for those. Be present!

Those people who are in your life right now are there for a reason, either to teach you something or to offer gifts to you. It's easy to get caught up in the turmoil, in the drama, in the problems of life, but don't let that distract you from the moment you are in right now.

Look around right now and see where you are, who you're with, what you're thinking about, and just *be*. Enjoy the moment, wherever you may be. Give the people you're with your full attention, and if you are by yourself, notice the stillness of the silence. You can always be present *now*. Just know that whenever you are present and content with right now, you receive a gift to yourself and create memories to enjoy.

In other words, get your head in the game! The more you focus on right now, the more your problems and stress will fade away. We only stress and get anxious when we think about what *could* happen, and it's usually future thinking. Or we stress and get depressed when we think about what *did* happen in the past.

When we pay attention to *right now*, we don't stress about anything that could potentially be a problem in the future. Although it's important to learn from the past and have a vision for the future, it is also crucial to remember that we only have today, we only have right now, and nothing in the future is guaranteed. So let's make the most of the moment.

My encouragement for you is that you consider life a valuable gift, a present that is nothing more than what it is: the present. If you can keep your attention on what is happening right now, you will experience deep contentment and gratification that life is okay and that you will be just fine.

Learn from your past, plan for the future, and live in the now.

Chapter 14

---◆---

Walking Through the Wall of Resistance

"Okay, I can do this, I can do this, I can do this."

Other voice in your head: "No you can't. Who do you think you are? Just sit down, this is more comfortable for you."

"But I know I could do this, I know how good I am at this!"

Other voice in your head: "You're lying. You are worth nothing, and you'll never amount to anything. It's way too hard."

"I believe in myself. I know deep in my heart this is what I was meant to do."

Other voice in your head: "Just sit back down, you're afraid of change. You'll be rejected anyway."

"Shut up! I believe in myself, and I know I will become the person I need to be. I will do whatever it takes to fulfill my dreams. I *can* do this, I *will* do this, and I *am* doing this!"

These two voices are very present in our minds and are constantly working against one another, even when we don't know it. One is called *love* and the other is called *fear*. This is the primary reason we make one decision over the other in our lives.

Which voice is more prominent in your life? For a big portion of my life, fear drove me the most. Fear drove me to work like a dog in high school so that I could save enough money to move out by the age of seventeen. Fear drove me to excel in all of my jobs faster than anybody, but I was always feeling worn out, tired, scared, overwhelmed, and anxious just to prove that I was okay.

I still have to calm myself down from time to time to center my mind and realize who is talking to me in my head. Picture both of these voices playing tug of war within your own mind. They are battling for your attention and action.

Love and *fear*—these two words are very different. One wants you to fail and be miserable, and the other wants you to step out, take chances, be kind, and follow your heart. You may know what this inner struggle feels like. Have you ever had a moment when you were faced with a decision, and you knew deep down that you shouldn't make one particular choice but you did it anyway?

Maybe it was when you were with your friends, or looking at or doing something you shouldn't be looking at or doing, but you did it anyway. Those are the voices I'm talking about. They have consequences. These voices are keeping you from walking through the wall of resistance.

How can we follow our purpose? How can we love? How can we use technology as a resource? How can we be successful? How can we have what our hearts truly desire? How can we take risks and take chances? How can we have relationships and friendships with others? *By walking though the wall of resistance.*

This resistance is fear of change. This resistance is all those voices telling us that we can't do something, and we're listening to them. This resistance is fear of loving ourselves and becoming what we know we need to be. It's as if we go to open a door and our hand is on the doorknob, but we can't seem to turn it. Something is telling us not to; something is holding us back. It's when we go to eat three cookies when we know we should probably just have one. It's when our parents tell us to do something and we ignore them. It's when we have careers down the road and we find out it is not what we want to do, but we stay anyway out of fear of doing what we love.

There are so many examples. I could list reasons forever about why we won't or think we can't do something. I am not _____ enough—fill in the blank. I am not *thin* enough, I am not *in shape* enough, I am not *good* enough at this sport, I am not *pretty* enough, I am not *smart* enough, I am not *old* enough, and the list goes on and on. Whatever we keep telling ourselves and whatever we believe to be true is simply a lie. It's an excuse we keep telling ourselves so that we don't have to take chances, so we don't have to change, and so someone else can take care of us.

That is why I call it the wall of resistance. We come so far and then we stop at this wall. We don't know how to move it, and it blocks us from continuing down our own journey.

The Story of Siddhartha

Have any of you ever heard the story of Siddhartha? Regardless of your religious beliefs, there is something to learn from every story. I'll summarize it for you here.

Siddhartha was a young boy born in a huge palace. His family was shaping him to be king of many nations, so they wanted to protect him from the harm of the world and make him happy. They gave him everything and anything he asked for: any type of food, girls, parties, clothes, luxury—you name it, he had it all.

When it rained outside, they would keep him inside and shelter him and bring everything to him. He was literally raised in a perfect world; his family wanted no harm to ever be done to him. One day, when he had gone to the market with people from his castle, he noticed suffering in the streets, things he had never witnessed before. He became fascinated with the question, "How do you stop suffering?" He started obsessing over the question, "Why do people suffer and how can you fix it?"

As time passed, Siddhartha married a beautiful woman and they had a baby together. One night, he was to sneak out and set out on a journey to discover the answer to his question. He said he couldn't hold his child one last time because he knew he would never put him down. It was one of the hardest things he had to do, but he knew in his heart he had to find the answer to his question.

So he set out on a journey, and the adventure wasn't so fulfilling for him at first. He spent many nights in dangerous forests and had to beg for food at times. He had only the clothes on his back and no money, but he was determined to find his answer.

He met gurus of spiritual practices along the way and started to follow them and adopt their teachings to a T, which involved "no desire." Anything that was a worldly desire had to be cut off. This involved fasting, wearing barely any clothes, and engaging in long deep mediations. He continued this for a long time, hoping he would find an answer, but he still did not know how to stop suffering.

He was so deprived of the many things our bodies need that he was on the verge of death. Then one day, a wonderful lady gave him a bowl of rice and said, "Eat!" It was a godsend to him, and he took it and ate it. The gurus found out about this and shunned him from the crowd. He was on his own again, still searching for the answer.

He came upon a tree and declared, "I am not moving from this tree until I have my answer." So he meditated and meditated and started to really search inside himself. It was underneath that tree that he discovered the answer to his question. This stillness of silence brought an awakening, and he discovered that the answer to the suffering was inside us. He was then called the Buddha and was a well-known spiritual leader of his time, and he has helped hundreds of thousands get out of suffering and lead the lives they want.

Buddha would have never achieved what he had if he didn't walk through the wall of resistance. Do you think it was easy for him to leave his wife and child? Absolutely not, but he had to because he knew deep in his heart that he had a mission to fulfill. He was placed on this earth to do something. And what about God's son, the wise teacher, Jesus? He had to do the same thing. Do you think he enjoyed suffering on the cross? Do you think he liked being cast down by the words of others? No. But he knew in his heart that he had a purpose on this planet earth, and he wasn't going to let anything come in between.

Just ... like ... you ... and ... me.

We don't like resistance, but it can be our best friend. It can open doors to so many opportunities that we don't know are available to us.

When we face that trial, that suffering, that *fear*, we must stare it in the face and press on. Press on! Every success has come with doubt and with challenges, but it's what we do with those doubts and challenges that makes us the person we turn out to be. Walking through the wall of resistance means following your heart even when it seems as if everything is working against you: friends, parents, jobs, schools, everything.

Fear or Love?

Next time you find yourself facing a challenge, ask yourself, is this fear or is this love? Get to that silent place inside you where you can hear the answer.

We need to ask ourselves if fear or love is talking when we experience doubt. It is usually fear. This is such a powerful question to ask ourselves, because then we can get to the root of why we have or haven't done something. Once you've made your distinction, you are able to look fear right in the face and move forward anyway. One of the ways you can make the distinction is based upon how you are feeling. If a decision you are about to make has you feeling scared or overwhelmed, you're probably operating from fear. If the decision makes you come alive and feel joyful, then you are operating from love.

This is what I work on when I'm coaching someone. I believe the number-one feeling that holds us back from living the life we are destined to live is fear. Yet we were not born with hearts of fear, but of love. So I help my clients understand that although it is a lie, fear is frequently there and we must walk through it. When this happens, it is then that life starts.

Having the courage to stare fear right in the face and do what we want to do anyway is one of the most exhilarating feelings I've ever experienced. This is a high you could never find elsewhere. My best friend and I always view our problems as if we were "watching the show." What does this mean? It means being able to literally play your life on stage in your mind as if you are sitting in the audience watching everything happen.

Try it right now. Close your eyes and sit back in a comfortable position. Now I want you to picture one of your problems going on in your life right now, this very moment. But this time, pretend you are at the movies, and the movie you are viewing is your "problem." Picture everything: what you're wearing, who is with you, is someone yelling or laughing? See yourself onstage; see the situation going on. Now, see yourself in the audience watching this movie, eating popcorn and candy, and laughing with your friend.

Let's pretend it's a comedy show. Right now, you are just observing. You are the observer of what is going on in your life. How do you feel? Do you feel more relaxed? Maybe you feel like your problem isn't as crazy as it seems. The purpose of this is to view what is happening to you as "watching a show," the show of your life. I use this technique frequently. It helps me so much. It helps to take me out of the situation and able to literally watch and view my fears and problems as if they were being lived by someone else. When we do this, we don't associate our fears as something that we *are*, but rather a movie we have just watched.

One of my favorite books that helped me on my journey to self-acceptance and inspired my idea of "watching the show" is *Radical Acceptance* by Tara Brach. She sheds light on the awareness of the process of acceptance when she writes:

> What we experience as the "self" is an aggregate of familiar thoughts, emotions and patterns of behavior. The mind binds these together, creating a story about a personal, individual entity that has continuity through time. Everything we experience is subsumed into this story of self and becomes *my* experience. *I* am afraid.[9]

My understanding of her thought is that when we rehearse our problems over and over again in our minds, or when we rehearse our fears, they begin to be something that we associate with as something that we *are*, instead of something that we may just be going through at the time. This is where we run into trouble, because we start to view our fear as something that is a part of us. That is why it feels so real. When we are able to view our fear as

---

9 Tara Brach, *Radical Acceptance* (New York: Bantam Dell, 2003), 19.

something we see onstage—something that can be seen, laughed at, and then left at the movies—we can move forward in our lives, leaving fear in the dust.

How Do You Overcome Fear?

Always remember that fear is a lie. I know I've said that before in previous chapters, but it's worth repeating over and over again. Fear is an illusion. It is created by our own mind, and yet it seems so real. It appears so scary within us that, if we were to take the first step, it would be one of the hardest things we had to do. I am not going to downplay how prevalent fear is in our lives. It's there and it's knocking. It wants you to fall flat on your face; it wants you to stop loving and start hiding. Please hear me when I plead, we are simply created to love. To love ourselves and to love others. How do you overcome fear?

- "I just do my very best. I know that everything that everyone throws at me I won't be able to do. I think it is very important to ask for help."—Maeghan, 24
- "Repetition. Keep doing what you are afraid of. Eventually it will become more natural for you."—Hero, 26

Next time you feel fear, when fear is so present that you shut down, remember that it is a lie and that you are the one creating the fear in your mind. Fear isn't something that can be touched; therefore, it is not real. A friend of mine brought up a fantastic point: What happens once you have that momentum of successes coming? When everything seems to be working out and you're having a great time, then *bam!* A challenge comes your way and you hit that wall of resistance again.

What do we do? It happens to all of us. We have setbacks, hurdles, and walls that we are going to face. Do we give in and say, "Maybe next time?" or do we say, "No, not this time! Lies, you're not going to get me this time!" We usually shut down our true voice that tells us to take that next step and keep going, even though we want to give up—especially when it would be much easier to give up.

Here are some words from another millennial, Hero, age 26, who shared some great insight with us. I asked him, "How do you pick yourself up after you have hit a major setback and some technicality gets in the way? How do you get yourself together and find the energy to get back on track?" His replies:

- "I think it's different for everybody, and that is where you find out the most about yourself. And you have to really dig deep within yourself to find the answer. It also depends on the individual."
- "For me, personally, I am firm believer that time heals all and that with time everything becomes better. No matter what."
- "Everything in this entire world revolves around time. It just keeps moving forward, a momentum that you cannot stop no matter what. It is a vehicle that will take you past the point of the setback."

I think Hero offers great advice when he tells us to look inside ourselves and admit that fear is different for everyone, because it is. My encouragement to you is to find out what that means for you and follow that. Whether it is an inspirational video, a song, a person, a quote, or a workout, use it to get back on track because you are made for something amazing. Tap into the inner part in you that says, "Go for it. Take that step."

Just remember, you are more than what you see yourself to be. You were made to do something far greater than fear will ever tell you. When those many voices come rushing into your mind like a wave, listen to that one voice that says you *can* do this and that you were *made* for this! Don't listen to the voice of fear; listen to *your* voice—the real voice. And don't forget to get your popcorn and watch the show. Step forward, open the door, and break down your wall of resistance.

Chapter 15

Wake Up to the World around You

Notice all the beauty that is right there waiting for you to see!

Someone once told me, "You're alive, Hailey, but you're not living." I wasn't too sure how to take that. Was that advice or was that criticism? Whatever it was at the time, it stuck with me, and as I got older and more mature, I started to view it as the best piece of advice I had ever received. I really want to share with you how I have interpreted this information and how much it has helped my life.

I thought to myself, *How could I be alive and not living? That doesn't make much sense to me.* When I finally realized what it meant I was moved, inspired, and captivated. Waking up to the world around you means being alive for every moment of your life and, most importantly, noticing the beauty of the world. Our society is so poisoned with bad news and bad things happening. There is *always* a problem to find if you're looking for it. What I'm offering is a new perspective, a new way of viewing the world we live in.

Looking at something beautiful is different for everyone. Each and every one of you holding this book defines beauty as something different. It could be a painting, a sunset, an ocean, a couple in love, your favorite sports team winning a big game, a standing ovation at a concert, or anything else that to you defines what can be known as *simple beauty*. Have you ever heard the expression, "It's the little things in life that matter the most"? That really has been very true for the majority of my life, and I am so glad to be sharing all of this with you.

It's so easy to overlook beauty in our day-to-day lives and not open our eyes to the abundance and freshness of life. For example, my best friend and I love to watch movies. We are always searching and waiting for the next great one to watch. It is a form of relaxation. And it's funny because sometimes we have completely different tastes in movies, mostly because there is a forty-eight-year gap in our ages. And, yes, you're right. Nobody knows what to do with us!

But to continue my story, I usually don't like to watch older films. I like to watch newer and exciting movies. One day, my best friend asked if I wanted to watch the movie *Life is Beautiful*. I asked if it was an older movie and she said, "Oh yeah."

Well, I had agreed to it, but I wasn't too thrilled. A few minutes later it clicked! As I was finishing drying my hair, it dawned on me that this was the next chapter I was going to write about in my book. So I said, "Hailey, *Life is Beautiful* sounds like a great name for a movie, and I bet you can at least learn one new thing and share it in your book."

So I grabbed my notepad on my phone, sat down, and took notes as I watched the movie. It was an older movie, and not only that, it had subtitles! I braced myself and stuck with it, because I knew I could benefit.

The title of this movie is the very essence of this chapter: that our world is beautiful and that our lives can be beautiful if we just open our eyes to it even in the most troubled situations. You can find beauty in anything that you look at if you just search for it. You can see beauty in the most random places: in a car, sitting outside, in a great conversation; anywhere, you name it—it can be found. My hope for you is that from this chapter you start to open your eyes to all the precious moments in your life.

What Beauty Means to You

There's beauty in a sunset, there's beauty in a sunrise, there's beauty in a flower, there's beauty in a simple card you receive, and there is beauty in your smile. There is beauty in a crisp leaf that you step on as you're walking outside your door in the middle of fall, beauty in the first snowfall, and beauty in a young child saying his or her first words.

Beauty might mean to you something completely different than it means to me. Beauty can be seen and not heard; beauty can also be heard and not seen. It all depends on what you consider beauty to be. For you, it could be your favorite baseball team winning a World Series game; it could be watching a play, hearing someone sing, watching fireworks, seeing an old couple walk in the park who are still in love, seeing two people in love get married, a breathtaking photograph. I would encourage you to think about what you consider beauty to be.

Getting back to the movie, *Life is Beautiful*, made in 1997, revolves around the main actor, Guido, protecting his son's innocence after he and his family have been taken to the Nazi concentration camps. He protected the boy every step of the way by pretending that it was all a game and that if he didn't ask for food, and if he hid out all day and didn't say a word, he would end up winning a giant army tank.

In the middle of the concentration camps, where murder, starvation, hopelessness, and weakness existed, there was beauty, simply because the father radiated unconditional love for his son. He gave his son hope when there was despair. He ended up dying for his son, and the son went on to be saved and to be reunited with his mother. To me, a love like that is beautiful.

I have another example from when I was leaving an old waitress job. I wanted to suck all the knowledge I could from everyone before my last day. One of my managers really impacted my life when I asked him the question, "What advice do you have for me as I embark in my future career?" He looked at me, smiled, and said, "Come with me."

We went outside. It was a beautiful day out. The sun was shining, a light breeze hit my face, and I couldn't help but take in a big deep breath of fresh air because of how peaceful it was. Colorful flowers surrounded us as we walked by the parking lot. He looked at me, pointed to the sky and all around us, and said, in a gentle tone, "See this. Never forget to stop and smell the roses. Never forget to notice and appreciate the simple and beautiful things in life."

It has been two years since he told me that, and I have never forgotten and will never forget it. It's one of the best pieces of advice I have ever heard.

In that moment, I realized that people don't take the time to stop and appreciate the beauty in our world. We live in such a highly demanding, fast-paced society that it is very easy to speed to work and never once stop while we're at a red light to just notice what a nice day it is, or how amazing it is when the birds fly together in a flock. We need to just open our windows and take a deep breath and be grateful in that moment to be living for one more day.

Even though it is really hard to remember sometimes, I do it as often as I can. I forget too, I rush too, I am busy too, but I have made it a priority in my life to notice the little and beautiful things around me. It takes thirty seconds out of the day to stop, slow down, be grateful, and notice loveliness.

Having an appreciation of and waking up to the world around you opens your mind to all the possibilities in your life. It increases your gratefulness for living and helps you to not take life for granted. Everything—success, freedom, relationships—becomes more fulfilling when we offer gratitude for the things we have in our lives right now.

Gratitude is the center of everything we receive in life. Being grateful for who you are, what you have, and the people in your life is one of the most important messages in this book. The more grateful you are, the more you will receive. It is that simple. I kept a gratitude journal at first, until being grateful and saying thank you became a part of my life, and frequently I still write down all I have to be grateful for. However, keeping a gratitude journal is a great place to begin.

Life is such a precious gift, one we sometimes take for granted. Time never slows down, and we never get a second chance to live today. Our time on earth is over in a blink of an eye. Notice every bit of beauty that you can and don't let your life be such a big rush that you forget to stop and smell the roses and to appreciate all that you have.

I think Jon, one of the millennials I interviewed, gave great advice when I asked him what message he has for all of us:

> Slow down and relax a little bit. Everyone is so quick to achieve; just slow down a little bit. And that doesn't mean you don't work hard and give it 100 percent, but you need to understand there are more important things than grinding yourself out every single day.

The one thing that is extremely important is to seek out what is beautiful in every situation and have a grateful heart for what you have and what you desire in your life. It goes back to the old saying:

You can never have more,
if you don't appreciate
what you have first and foremost.

Chapter 16

Your Story Has Meaning

Life is a precious gift. We all need to make sure we unwrap and enjoy every bit of it.

My hope is that we don't forget to think big. Don't shut out that part of you that wants to achieve major things on a vast level. Our imagination is so powerful and this world can enable you to think small sometimes. Always dream big, and never forget your value and worth as a person.

You're story has tremendous significance in who you are. And you're still creating your beautiful story. There will be so many moments in your life when you feel scared, frustrated, disappointed, hurt, confused, and doubtful. Always remember there is a reason for whatever situation you're facing. It may make you stronger, wiser, or it might even be an inspiration to help another person out. Search for the lesson in what you are experiencing.

Where you're at right now is exactly where you are supposed to be: emotionally, mentally, physically and spiritually. So be easy on yourself, take the pressure off for being perfect and know your worth because you're completely worth it. I would encourage you to challenge yourself and learn something new every single day.

Consider that people will treat you the way you treat yourself. So be kind to yourself. And above all, let your life be "all about love." This is the message of this book. Never forget the power of <u>human connection</u>. Don't miss out on life because you're always on your cell phone. Be with the people you love and the ones who love you. Look them in the eye; give them your full presence. Love people, for they are doing the best they know how to do. People will make mistakes; don't disrespect them, show compassion and forgiveness because you mess up sometimes too.

It is easy to believe people who discourage us—especially if they are older or hold an authoritative position in our lives. What takes true power is to live out our dreams despite the criticism others give us.

Accepting yourself and other people for the way they are is something I work at everyday. Believe me it is not easy. But the irony of life is that if you know in your heart you are important you won't need to prove it to others, you will just live with love and joy. If you know in your heart you are successful you won't always need more and more things to prove it.

My friend Susan used to work as a Psychologist in the prison system. She would meet individually with the prisoners and help them turn their lives around. She said those people in there were so deprived of human connection that some of them would come in to see her just to shake her hand, for human touch. One person asked her, "Why do you love us so much?" She replied, "Because everyone is in their own prison; a self-imposed prison. The prison of how you think, your prison becomes your comfort zone, the prison of inadequacy. I love you because I don't see you any different than anyone else."

It is true; we are stuck inside of our own prisons until we can figure out a way not to be. That is how we need to see other people and ourselves, and know that we are doing the best that we can right now in this moment and so are they.

Always love; it is the answer to everything because people crave connection so much. Finally, know that every time you help another you are helping yourself. Have the courage to be vulnerable and love with everything you have every day, and you'll make more of a difference then you could ever possibly imagine.

The very last question I asked all the millennials I interviewed was, "What advice do you have for millennials around the world?" I asked this question because I want us all to understand that we are going through some of the same situations that were described in the story above.

We all have to go up against the same stereotypes. We all have to believe in ourselves. We all have to press forward when our fear is strong, and we all have to overcome our fear in order to experience the greatest successes and victories when we follow our passion. Here is some of their advice for all of us. These individuals really impacted my life in a powerful way, and I'm hoping that they will for you too:

- "The world we live in today is a broken world. You should not view life as the world wants us to, and if you shoot for a higher goal you will make it."—Erynn, 13
- "Things for us in this generation are not getting any easier. It's getting much harder, and because of that we need to be where we want to be. Life is going to be hard, but have an outline for your life. And even if things don't go as planned, still push yourself to achieve something. Keep pressing forward always."—Lonn, 24
- "To the millennials around the world: find a mentor, one who you can learn from and who is not of your generation and someone who will challenge you. Also, show respect for anyone and everyone that you meet; you never know how that person can help you in your life. I met this guy in an elevator and started conversation with him, showed him respect. He looked like a janitor but I later found out he was the COO of the company, and I swear the engagement I had with him was part of the reason I got the job."—Maeghan, 24

If ever you feel anxious, worried, or fearful of the future, take a deep breath and be quiet. You have all the answers you need within yourself if you will just be still and listen. Life is a test, and we have the answer key.

As you continue to read through the authentic advice from your peers, start thinking about something you would say to your friends. These individuals are from different cities in Michigan and some are from other states in America. Much of our generation goes through the same experiences, good or bad, and it doesn't matter where we live. We're here to help each other out. We can all be on one big team and share in our victories together. We can discover who we are and who we want to be with the support of our team. When we realize we are in this together, it gets a little bit easier, and we shift our mind-set from competition to unification.

- "Don't overthink about things. It just makes you stressed. Extract every moment from every experience that you can."—Mallory, 18
- "Don't listen to stereotypes, because they're not true. And find people and jobs that will help you succeed toward your own strengths."—Kara, 24
- Advice to other generations: "If you would treat us the way you treat other people, you would get so much more out of us. Realize that we can help you and we want to help you. We have the creativity, we have the innovation, and we want to help!"—Kara
- "We don't want to disappoint; we want to please and take care of other people. But in the end if that doesn't make us happy, you have to love yourself if you're going to love anyone else."—Hero, 26
- "Do what makes you happy or what's best for you, because you cannot take care of anyone else if you don't take care of yourself first."—Heather, 19
- "Everyone needs to have that one thing that keeps them motivated to push through when you don't want to."—Hero, 26
- "Everything's going to be alright." –Sean, 33
- "You have one life. Live it, now." –Sean, 33
- "My only advice is that nothing is unattainable, but nothing will be handed to you. You actually have to put work in, face adversity, understand that you won't always succeed on your first try but you should always put yourself in the best situation to progress, improve and

be the best person you can be. Eventually you will find whatever success you are seeking." – Brandon, 32

Now you have many different pieces of advice you can dwell on and put where you can see their encouragement every day. Your toolbox is full now, and you have everything at your fingertips.

There may be many people telling us that we can't do what our hearts truly desire. Unfortunately, those voices may end up sticking with us (especially if we are young), but the voice that can be the loudest is our own voice of self-doubt. Trust that the decisions you make for your future are the right ones. Then check them out with your mentors, the people you trust who have your best interests at heart. You know yourself better than anyone on the planet, and you know deep down in your heart that you have what it takes and that you are a leader of this generation.

When you can't make a decision and you don't know what to do, follow your heart. When all the voices of other people are telling you not to do something, listen to *your* inner voice. When you are feeling overwhelmed, remember why you started in the first place. When you are on a roll of success and you hit a wall, be courageous enough to continue to press forward.

As I mentioned in the beginning of this book, you have your own story.

You are still creating that story, that story of meaning, of passion, of hopes, and of dreams.

That story has made you into who you are today. Your story has meaning, and you are the artist now. You hold the paintbrush and you can choose to paint the picture you have always dreamed. Your mind is powerful, and your imagination is strong.

Believe in your power, believe in your
vision, and believe in yourself.

When you do that, whatever you want will be yours. Don't forget to always be grateful. The more you give to others, the more you will get back.

I cannot always control what goes on outside.
But I can always control what goes on inside.
—Dr. Wayne Dyer

I am so excited to see what the future has for you. I want to hear all about your successes, your dreams, and your struggles. I really want to hear your input and help in anyway that I can!

Remember, we are all on one big team, so when we win, we win together. Let's help each other out, but start with ourselves! Now I feel this is the right time to ask: Did you get a millennial makeover? Live inspired, and live with love.

You can leave any of your comments about the book and/or questions about my coaching program, or just to stay connected.

My website: www.haileyjordanyatros.com
My twitter: @HaileyYatros
Facebook Page: Hailey Jordan Yatros
Instagram: @HaileyYatros
YouTube: Hailey Yatros

Books I Recommend all Millennials to Read:

Change Your Thoughts—Change Your Life, Dr. Wayne Dyer

The Greatest Miracle in the World, Og Mandino

Lovingkindness, Sharon Salzberg

The Four Agreements, Don Miguel Ruiz

Unlimited Power, Anthony Robbins

You Can Heal Your Life, Louise L. Hay

The Success Principals, Jack Canfield

The Noticer, Andy Andrews

Love, Leo Buscaglia

Change Your words, Change Your Life, Joyce Meyer

Everyday a Friday, Joel Olsteen

Born To Win, Muriel James, Ed.D., and Dorothy Jongeward, Ph.D.

The Power of Intention, Dr. Wayne Dyer

Captivating, John and Stasi Eldredge

Secrets of the Millionaire Mind, T. Harv Eker

The Charge, Brendon Burchard

The Shack, WM. Paul Young

The Bible, New Living Translation

Cross Roads, WM. Paul Young

Secrets of Six-Figure Women, Barbara Stanny

There's a Spiritual Solution to Every Problem, Dr. Wayne Dyer

A Far Cry from Home, Sandy Richards

A Year of Miracles: Daily Devotions and Reflections, Marianne Williamson

About the Author

A young millennial herself (20 yrs. old), Hailey's dreams and visions started early. Being the youngest in her class, at age 18 Hailey earned the Highest Award of Achievement in the legendary Dale Carnegie Course. Shortly after her graduation, she was offered a position to work at their company. She felt as if it was a great step towards her mission of helping young adults around the world. She went through an intense amount of training while working there; over 350 hours of preparation on her way to becoming a certified instructor. At age 19 Hailey had helped and coached hundreds of students' -from all ages-reach their vision. At the same time, attending The Union Institute and University full time. This past year Hailey says she has realized the magnitude of her purpose and decided her opportunities are infinite. Soon after Hailey left her position at

Dale Carnegie Training she began to put her passion into writing. She had such a strong desire to share with and encourage others to chase after their dreams. Hailey was working three jobs, going to school full time and writing a book; after a series of many sleepless nights, she had completed an entire manuscript in a month and a half. She also just recently became a mentor for the non-profit organization Reaching Higher leadership course that strives to help young adults achieve purpose. Her main driving force in life is fulfilling her mission and purpose. Ever since she was 13 years old she has had the same vision.

Hailey's purpose is to create leaders of the Millennial Generation also known as Generation Y, by breaking down the stereotypes that society has placed on them. She wants to help bridge the gap of the many generations ahead of her, including her own parents and show how Millennials can have better relationships with them. She wants to teach them how to LOVE & RESPECT themselves, whether it is by exercising, eating healthy, getting out of a broken relationship, reading, organizing their life, having more JOY in their life, switching their peer group, living in the moment, helping someone else through an act of kindness, or simply following their heart. Hailey's purpose is to live with an undeniable passion for life and to help others connect to THEIR passion and what they LOVE to do. Her main mission is to give young adults HOPE for their future and offer them a new perspective on life, showing them a new way to look at their challenges, or their dreams as if it were something they can have, and deserve to have!

Hailey was born and raised in the eastern part of Michigan. She has a big wonderful family of 9 and that is only counting under one roof! She didn't meet her biological father until the age of 15 only to find out that he lived just fifteen minutes away, her entire life. Many people call her an "old soul." But what Hailey calls herself is someone that earnestly seeks to be apart of a team, and to help grow that team – the Millennial team.

Within our ever-changing world, one thing stays the same; Hailey's undying love and acceptance she has for human beings.

CPSIA information can be obtained at www.ICGtesting.com
Printed in the USA
BVOW03s1535200214

345535BV00004B/4/P